Vintage Botanical Papers

VOLUME 1

End Papers, Junk Journals, Scrapbooking, Origami, Cut-Outs

BASED ON ILLUSTRATIONS BY MAURICE PILLARD VERNEUIL

2nd Edition

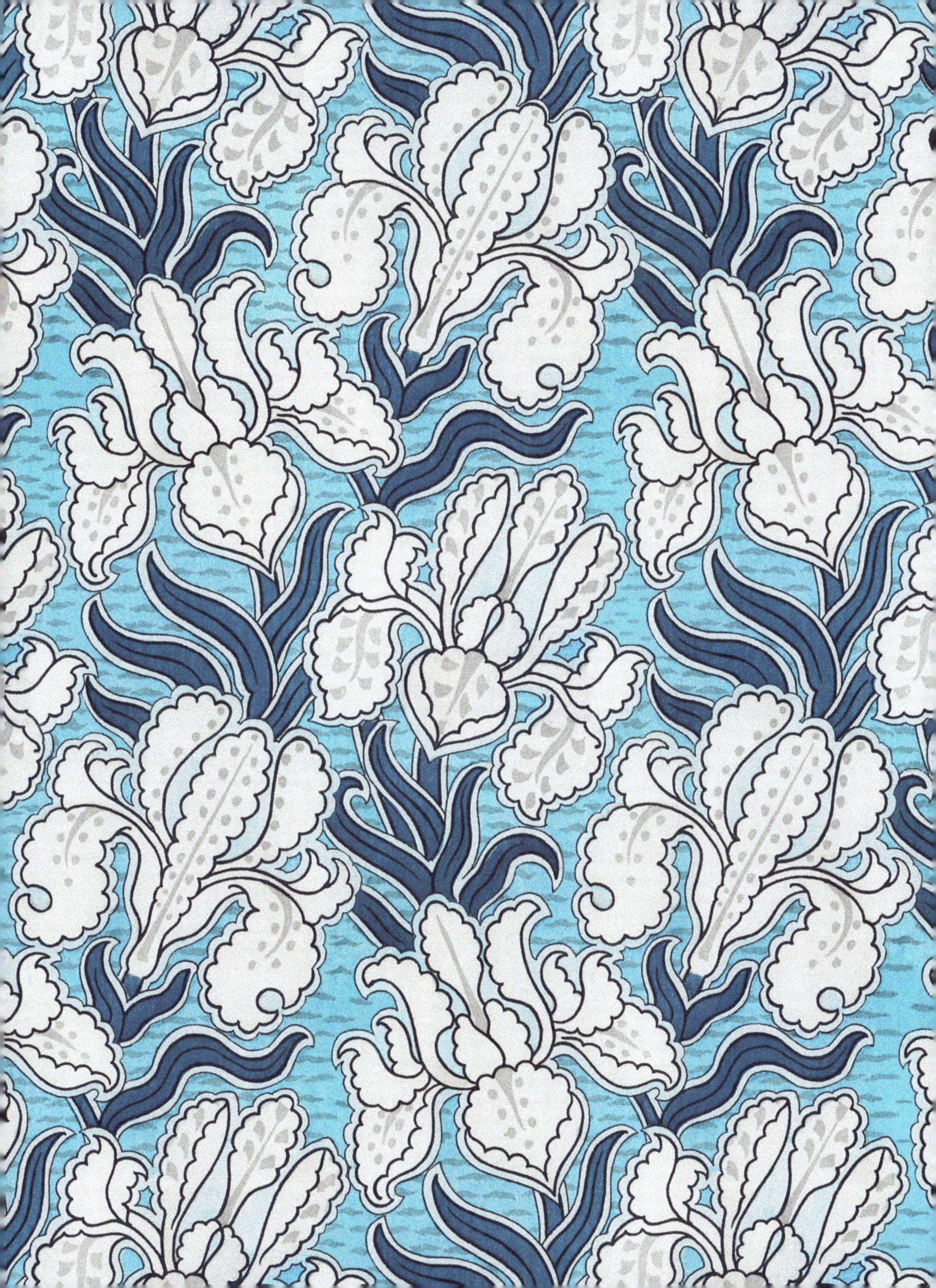

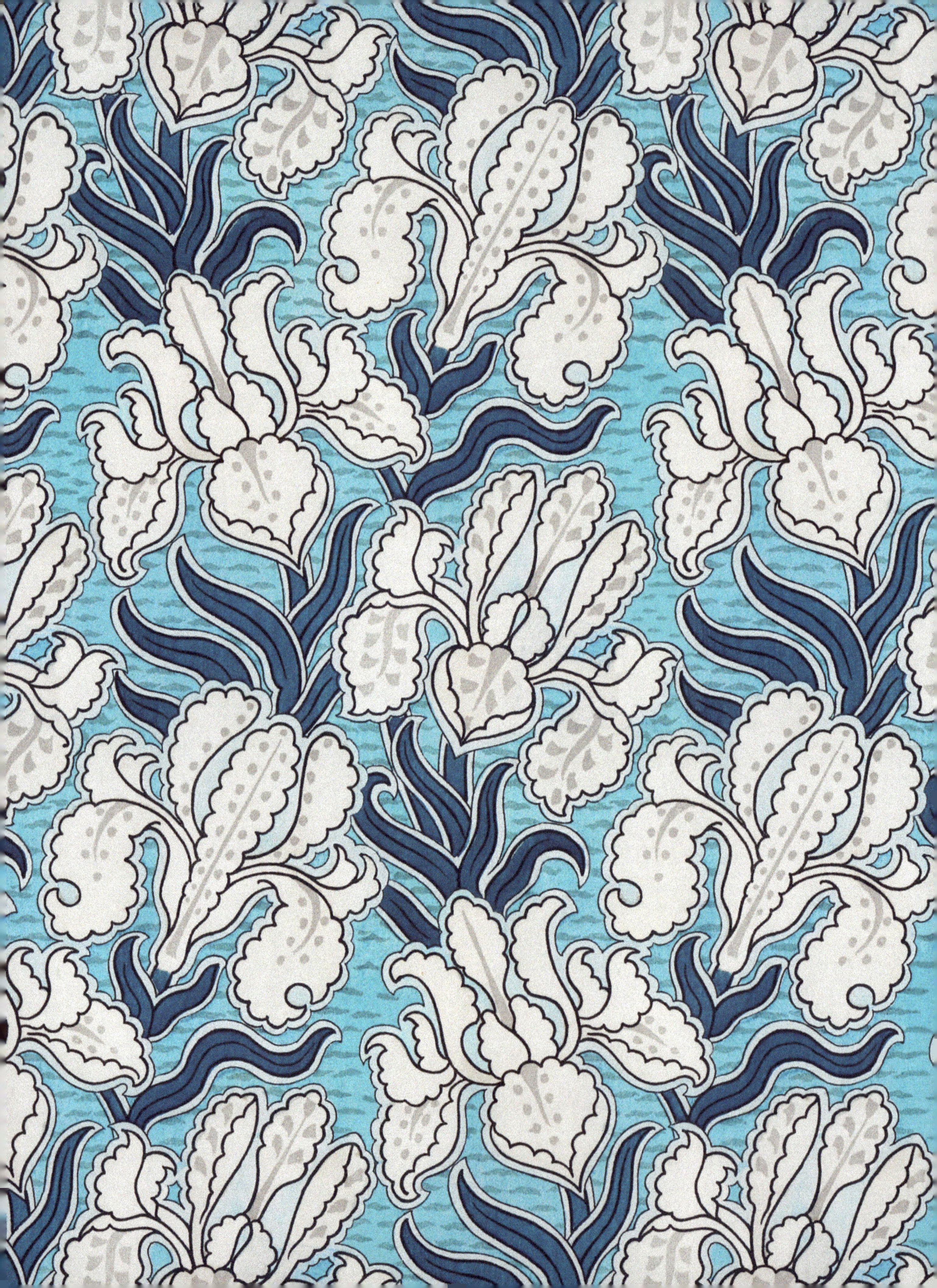

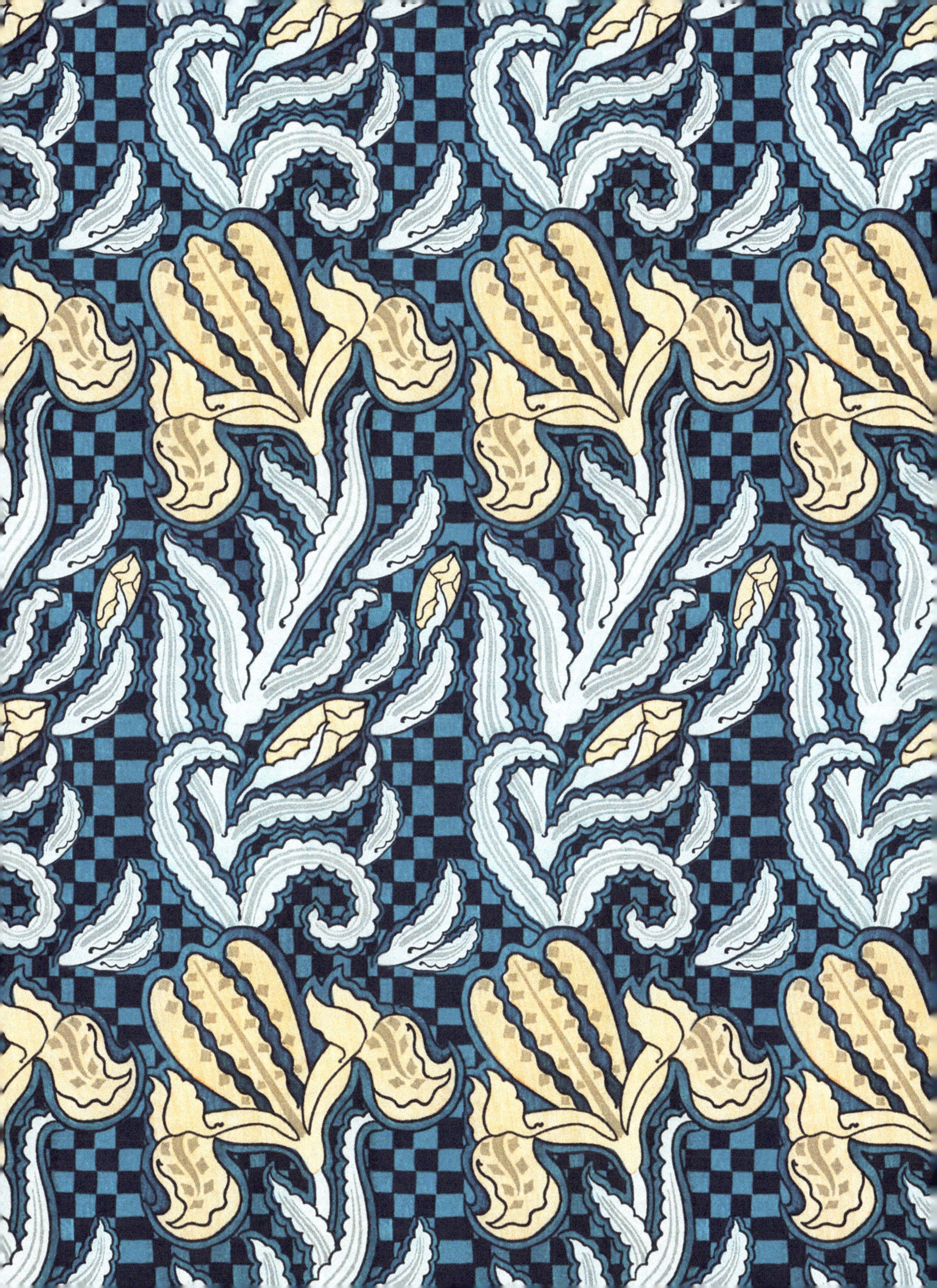

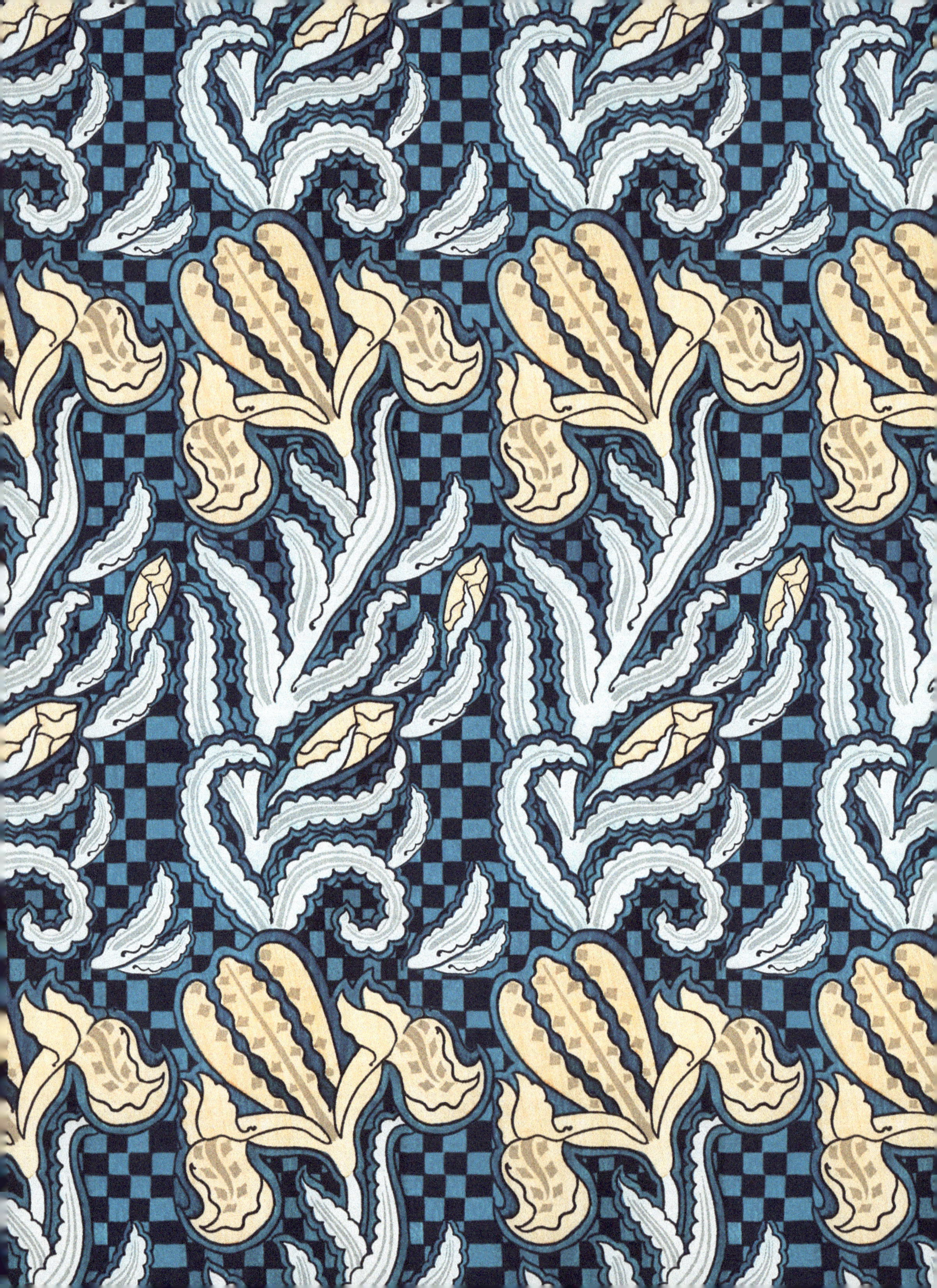

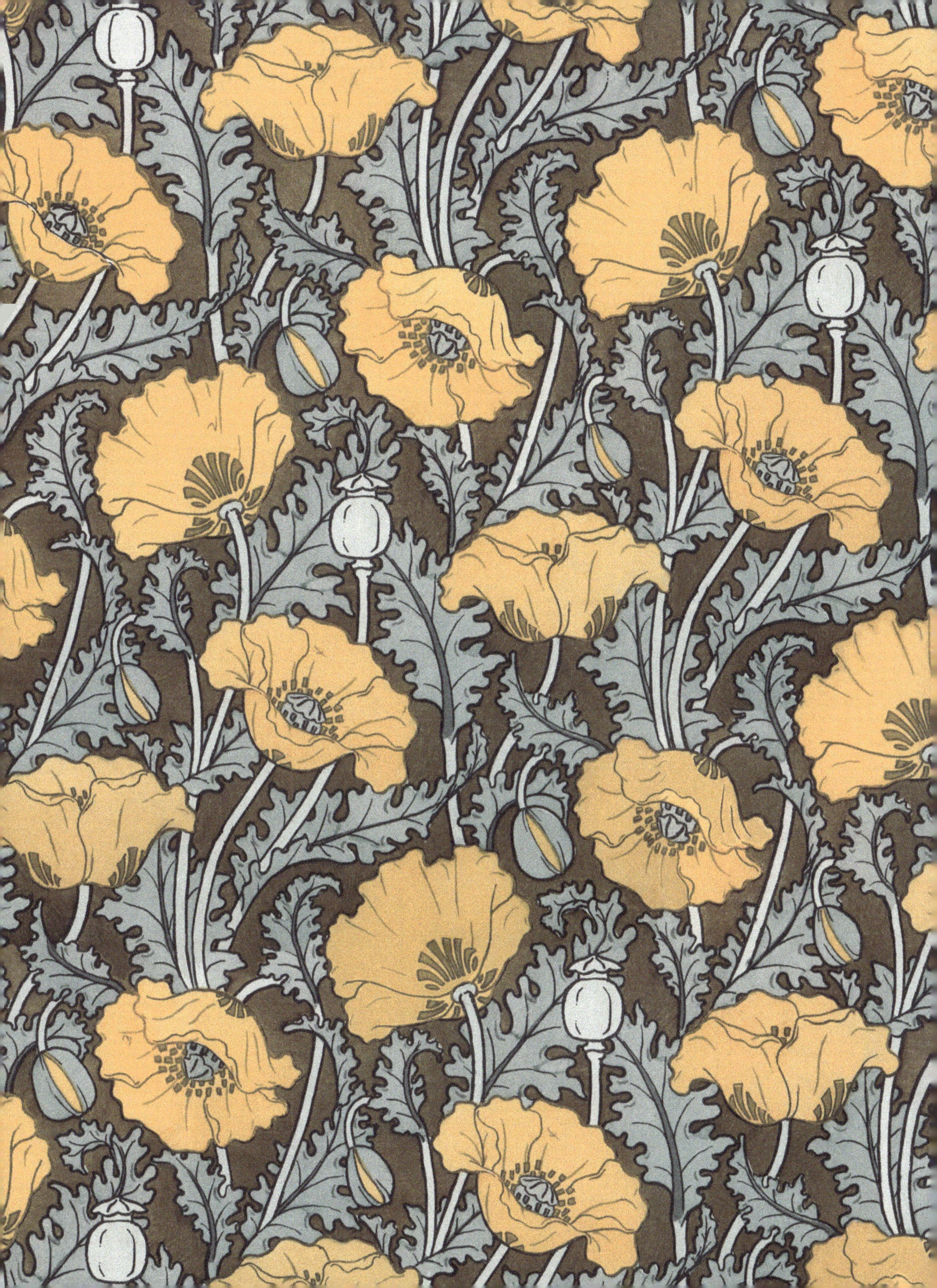

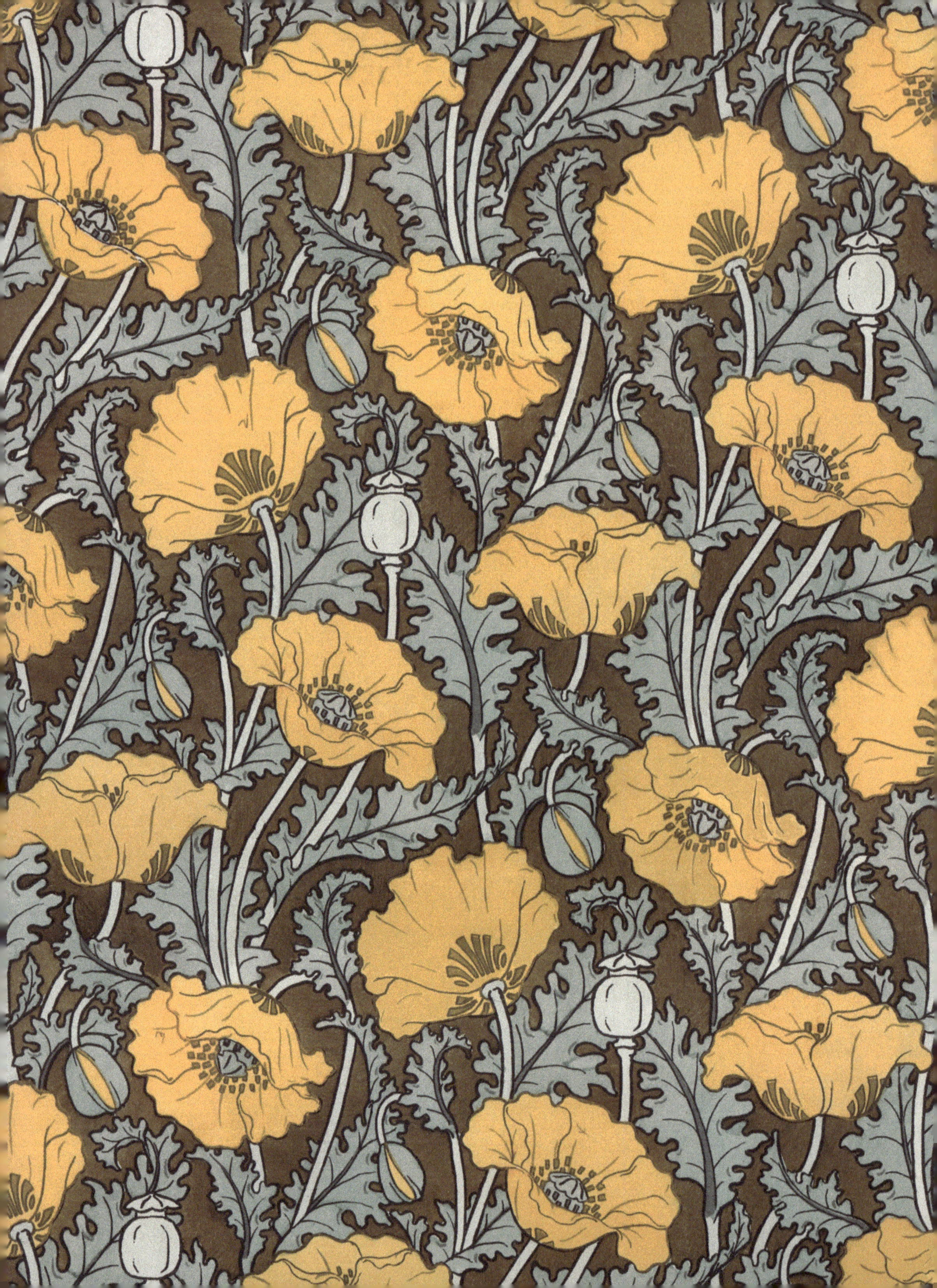

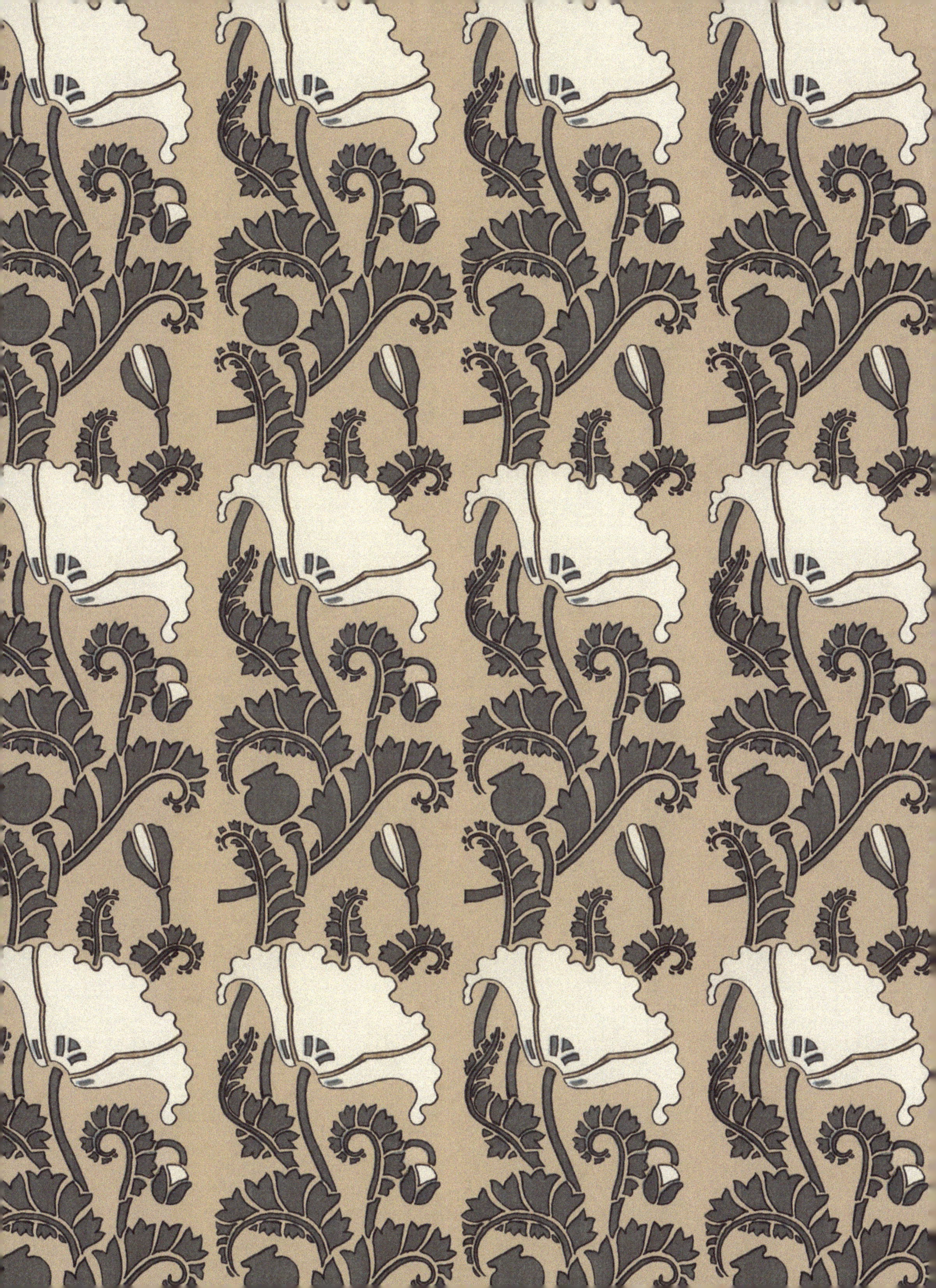

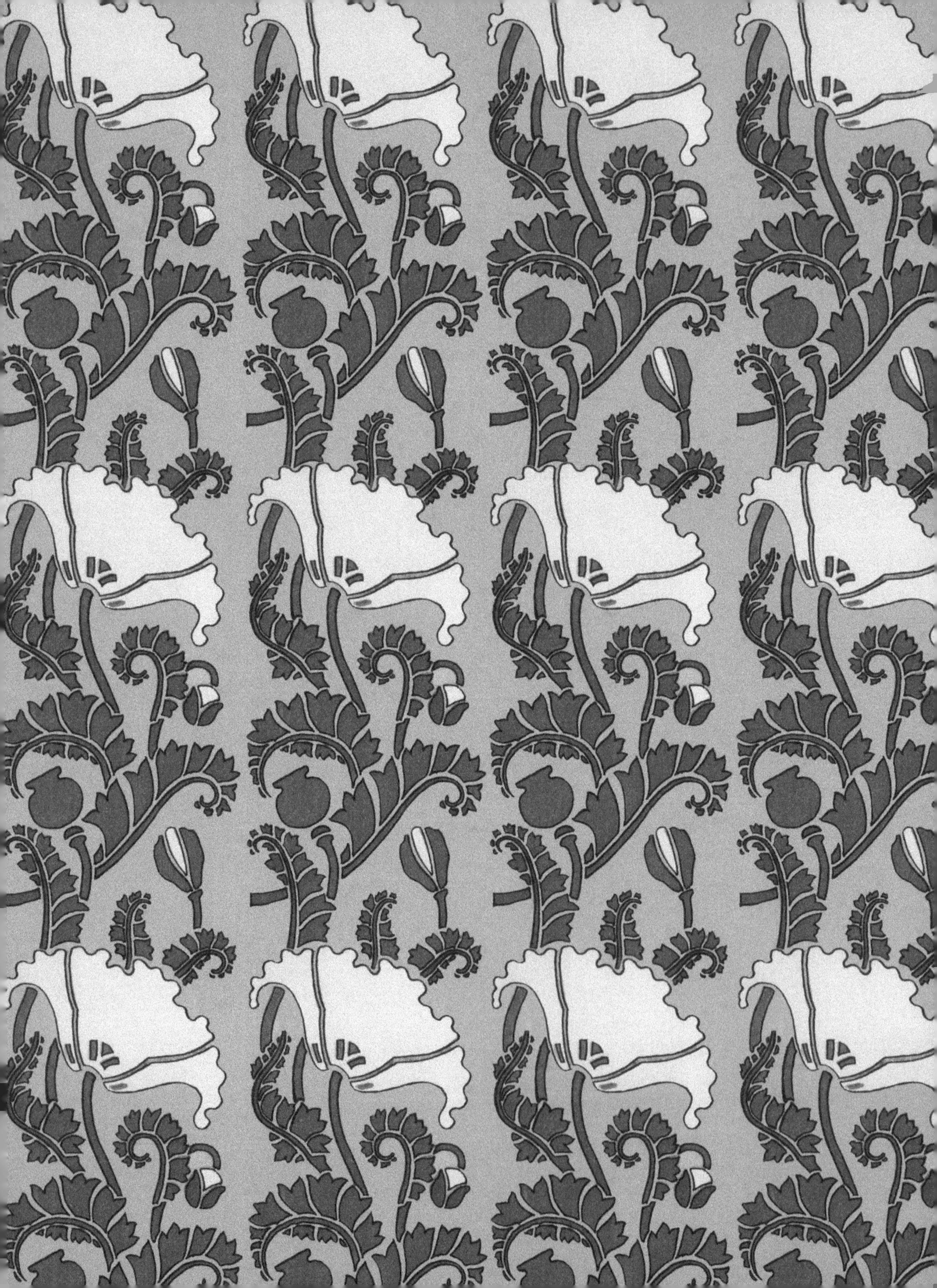

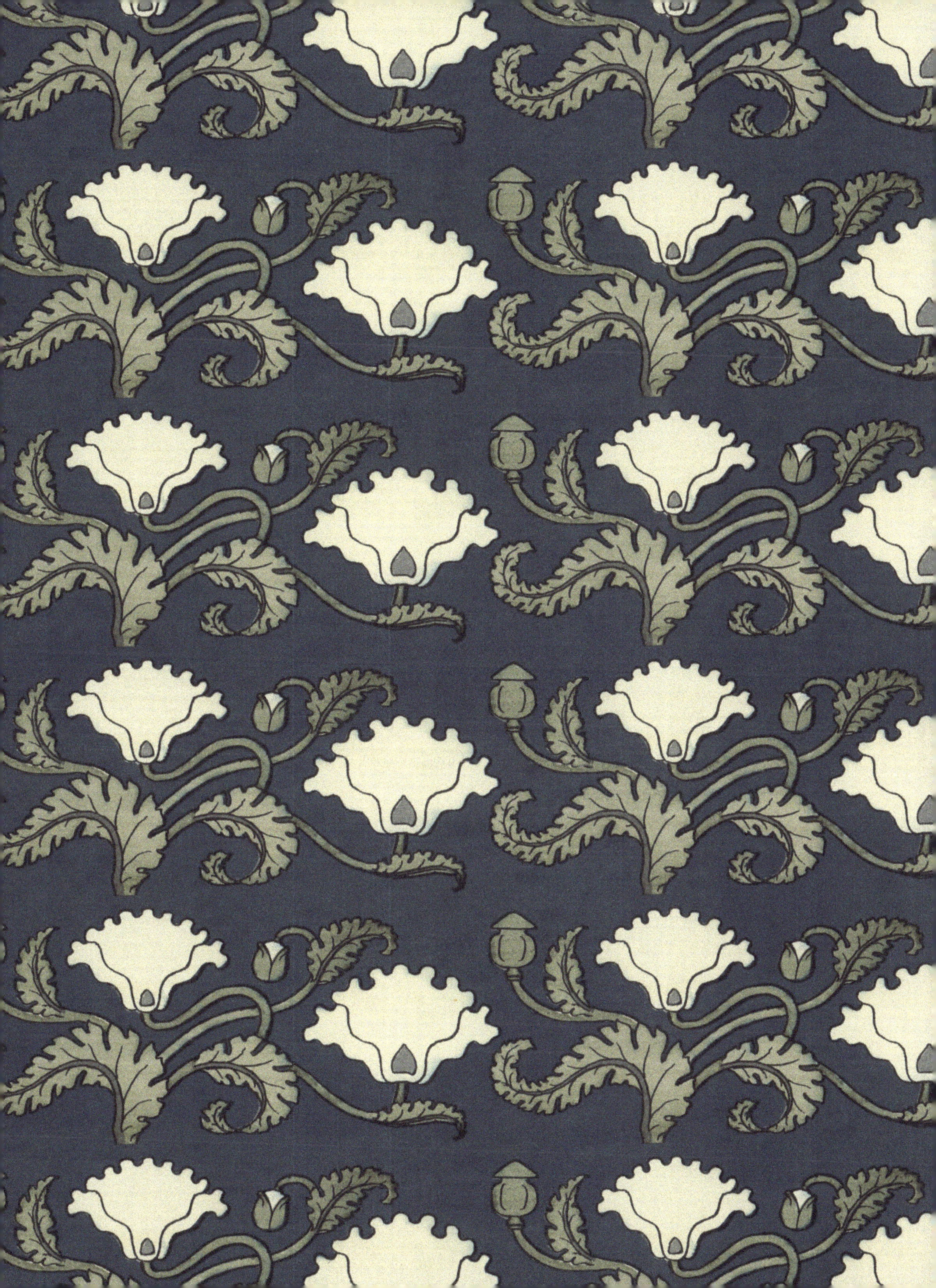

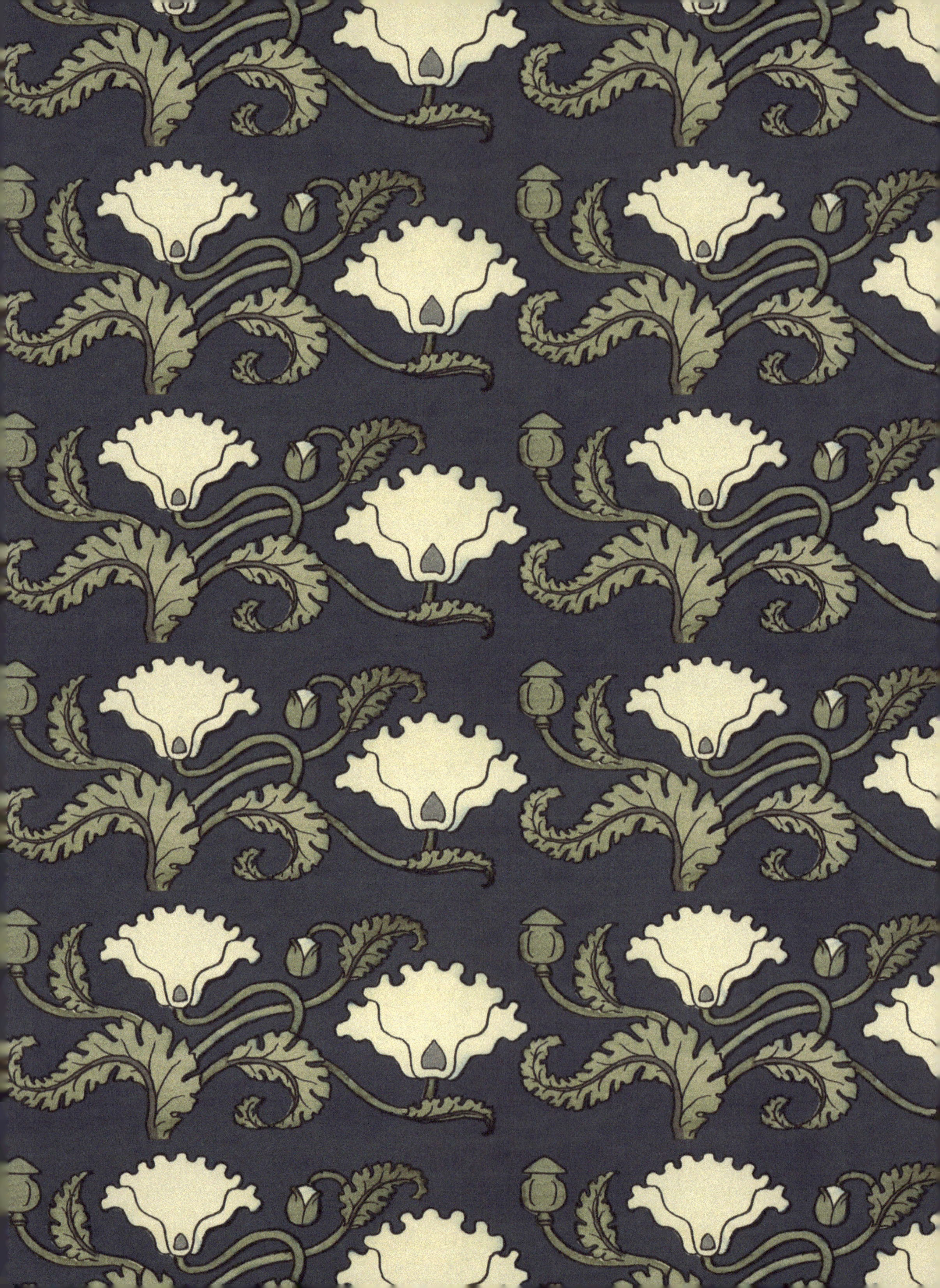

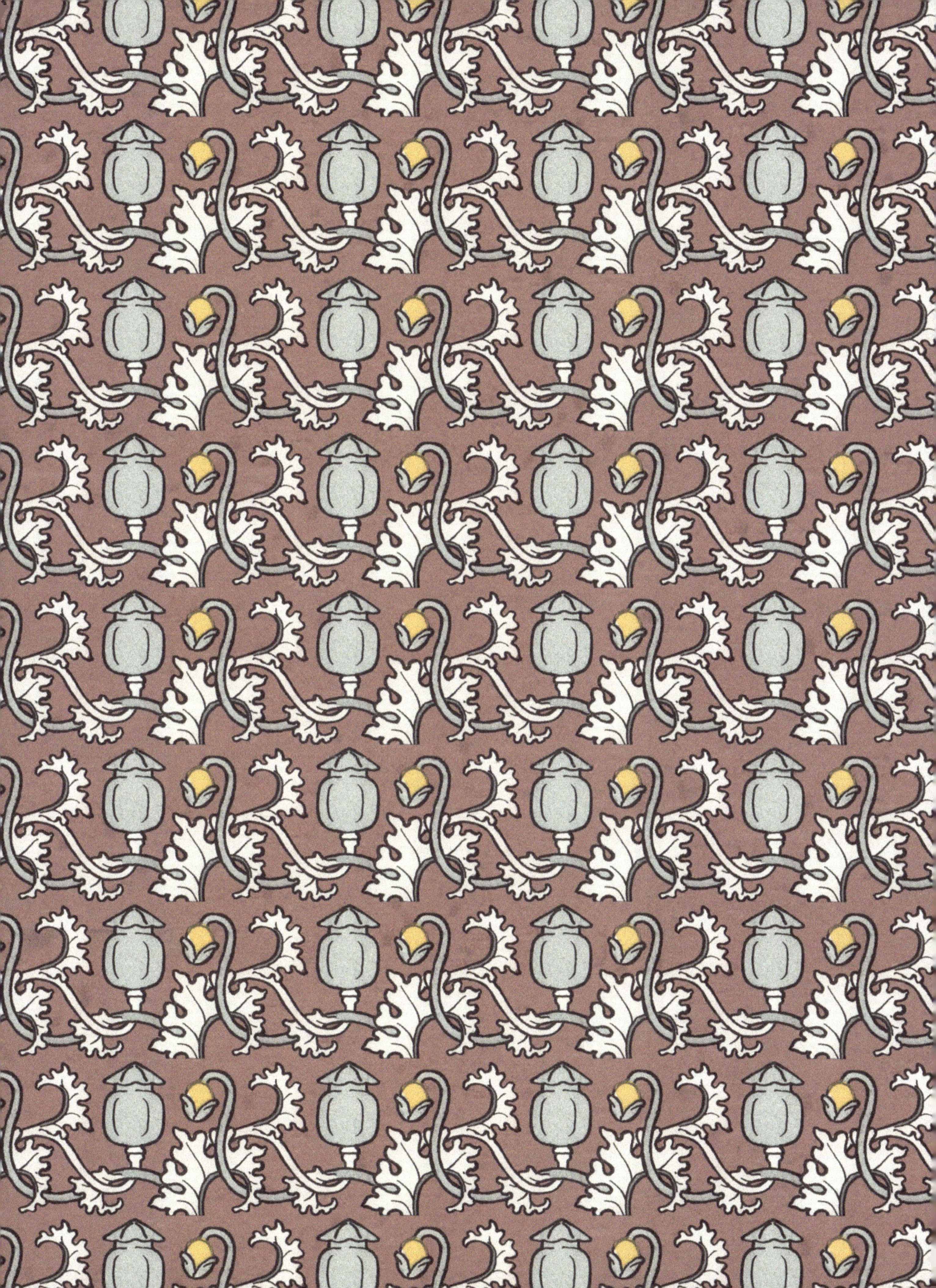

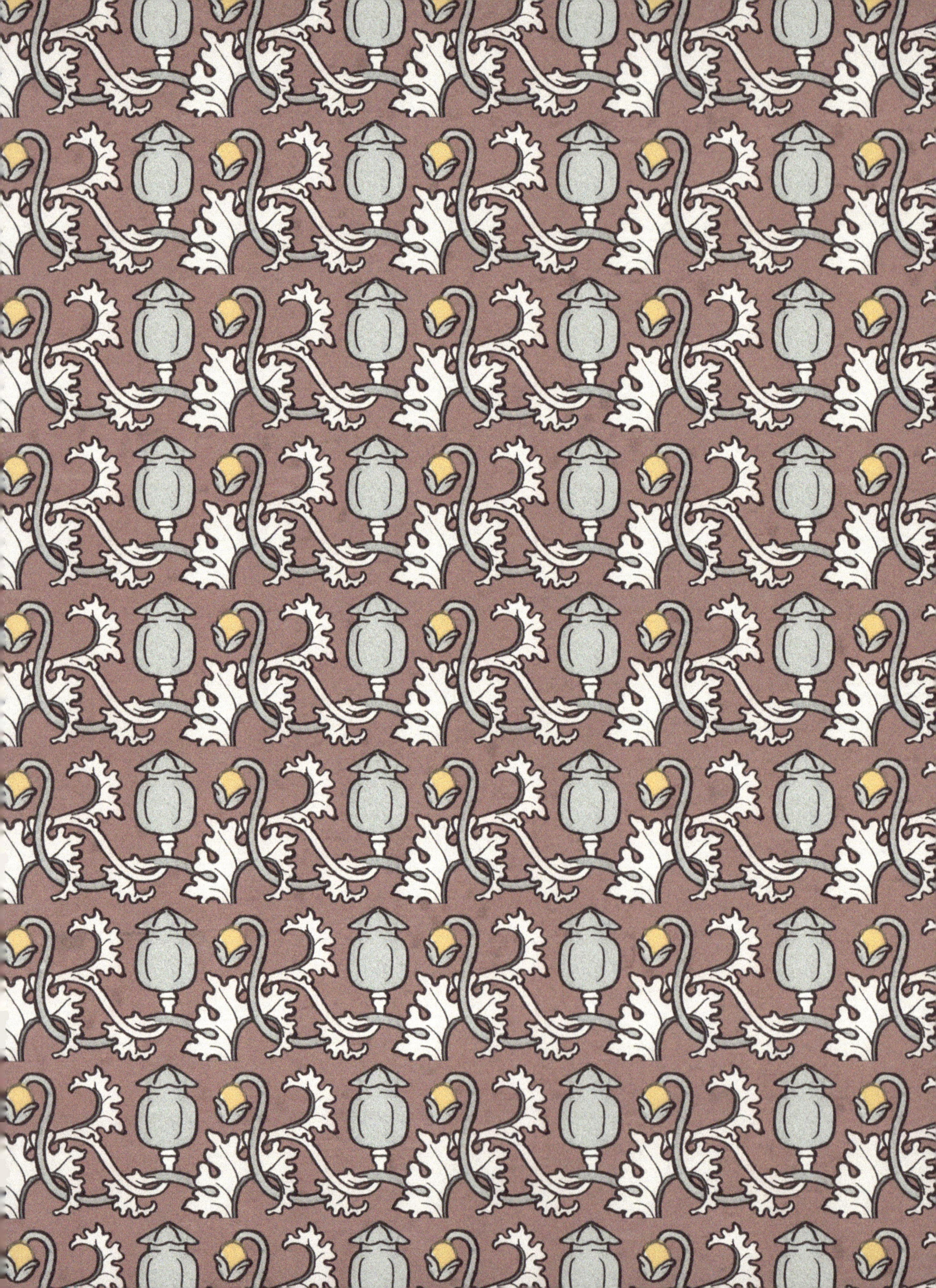

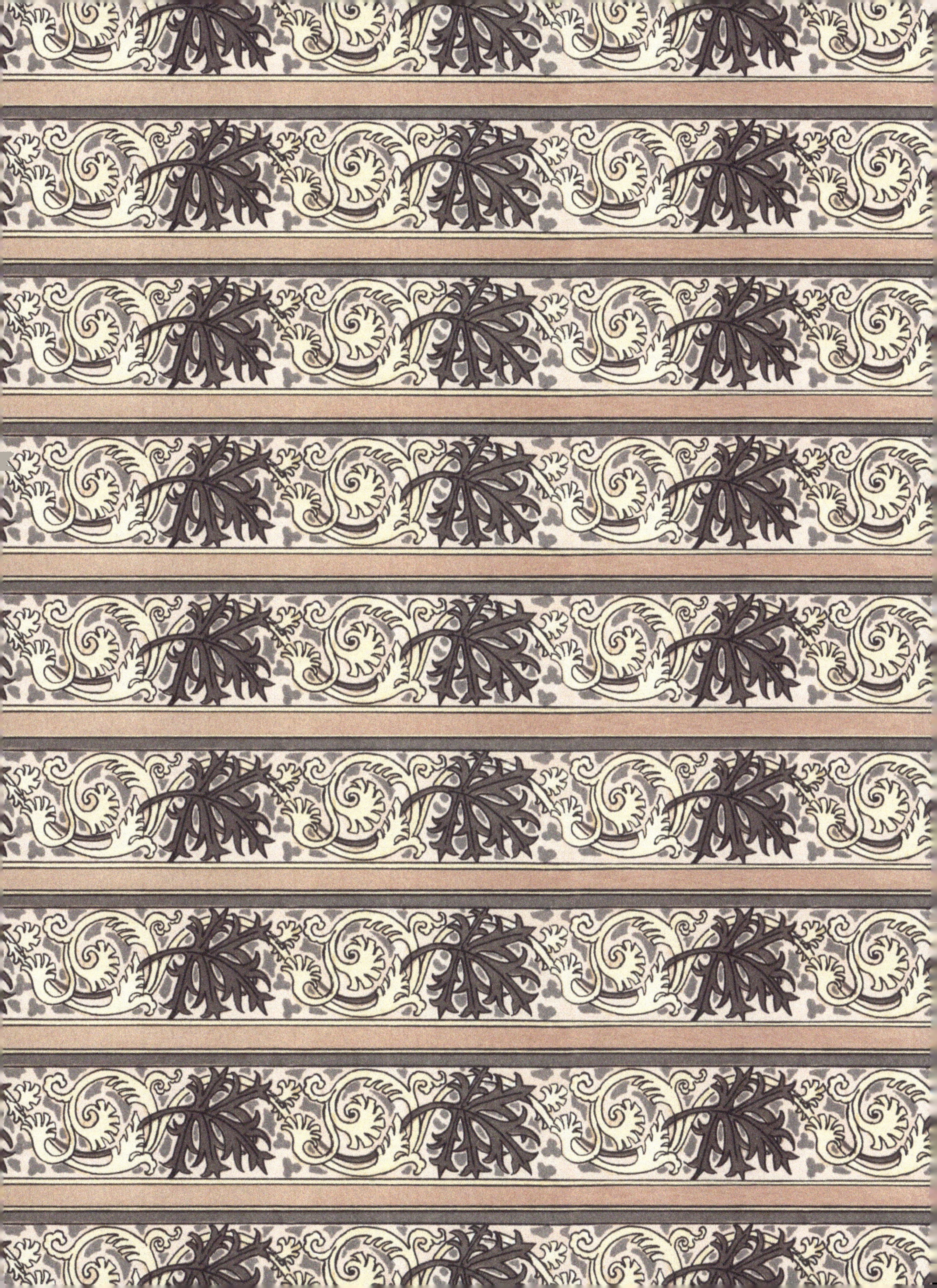

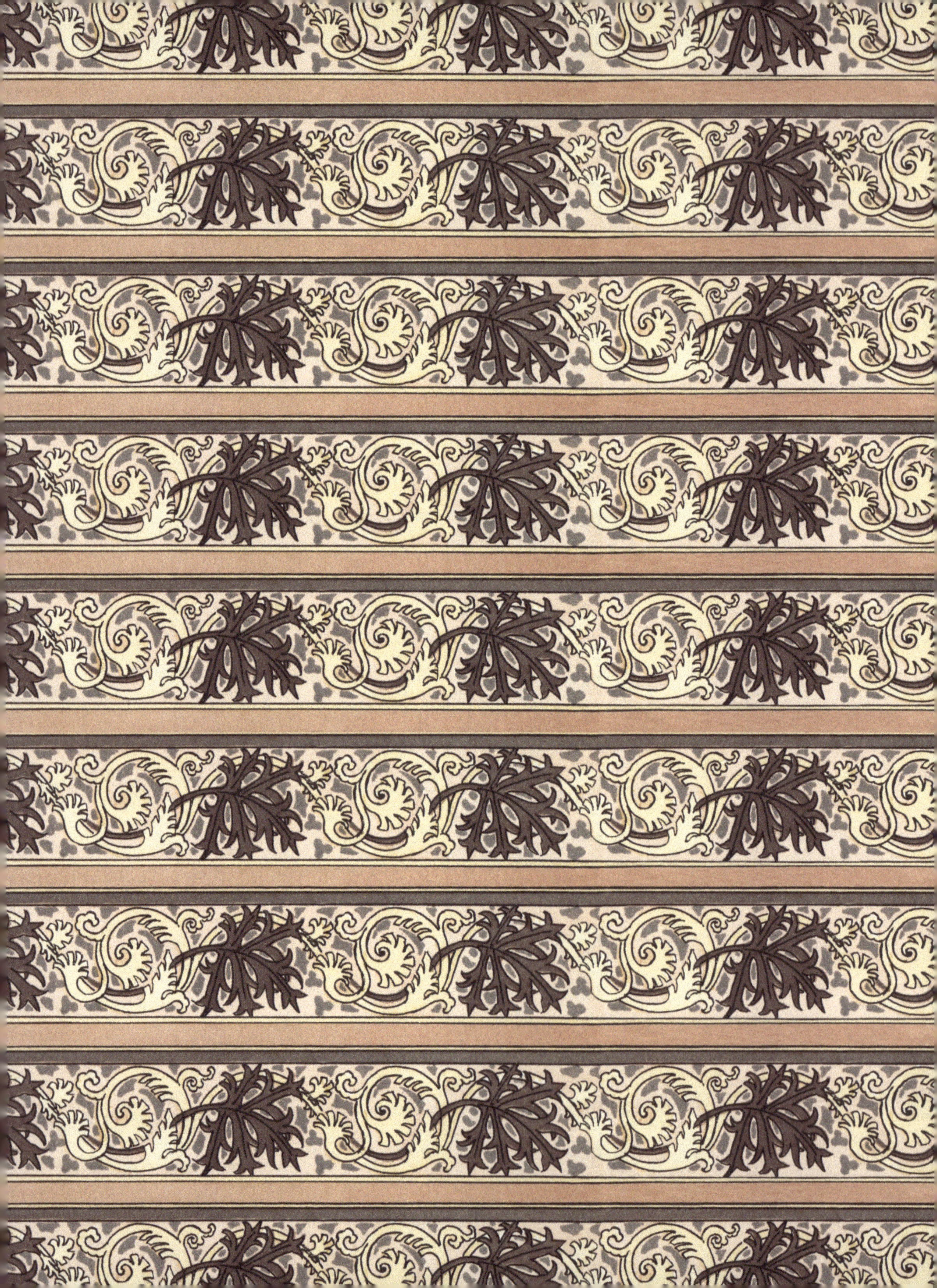

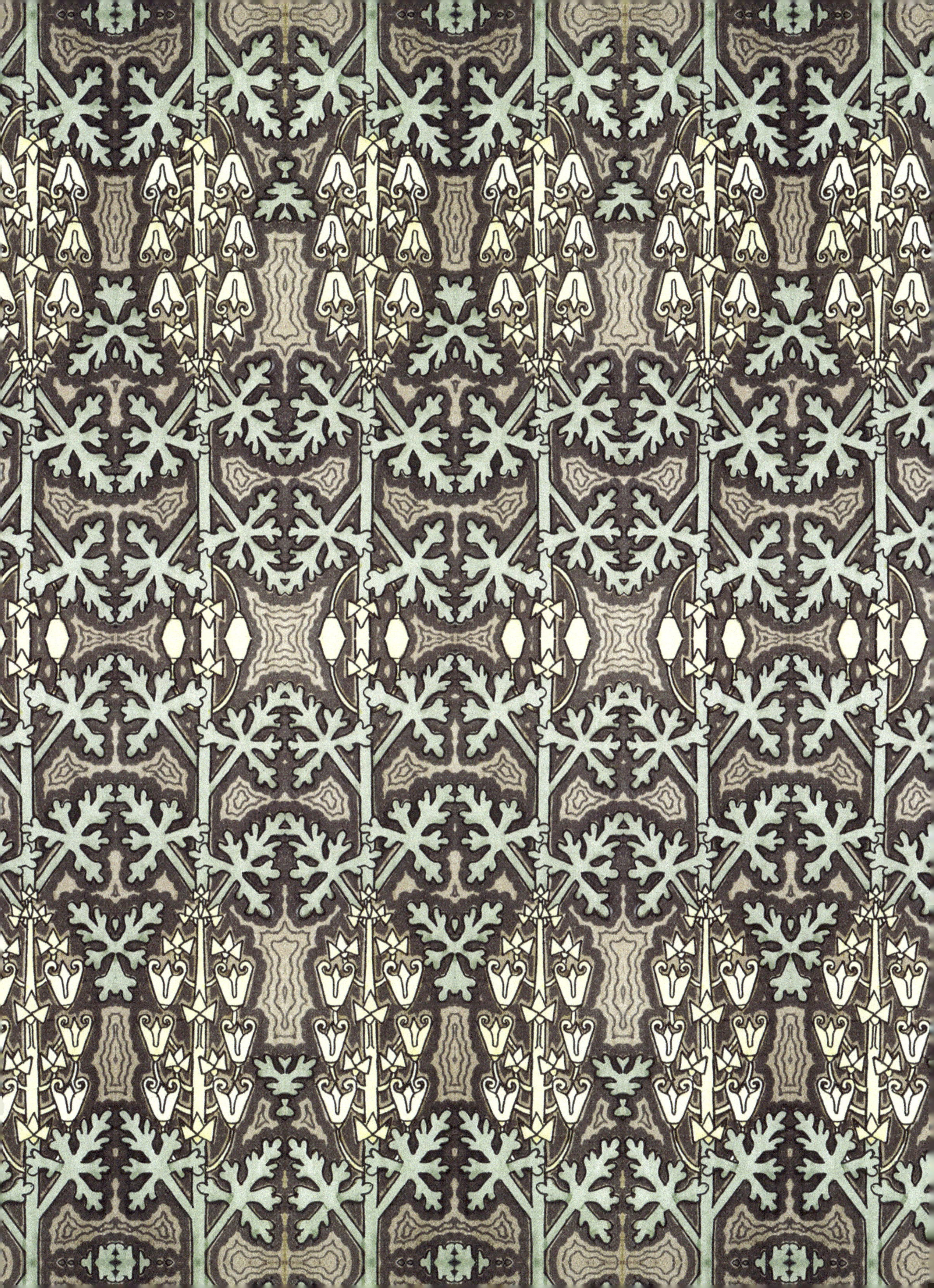

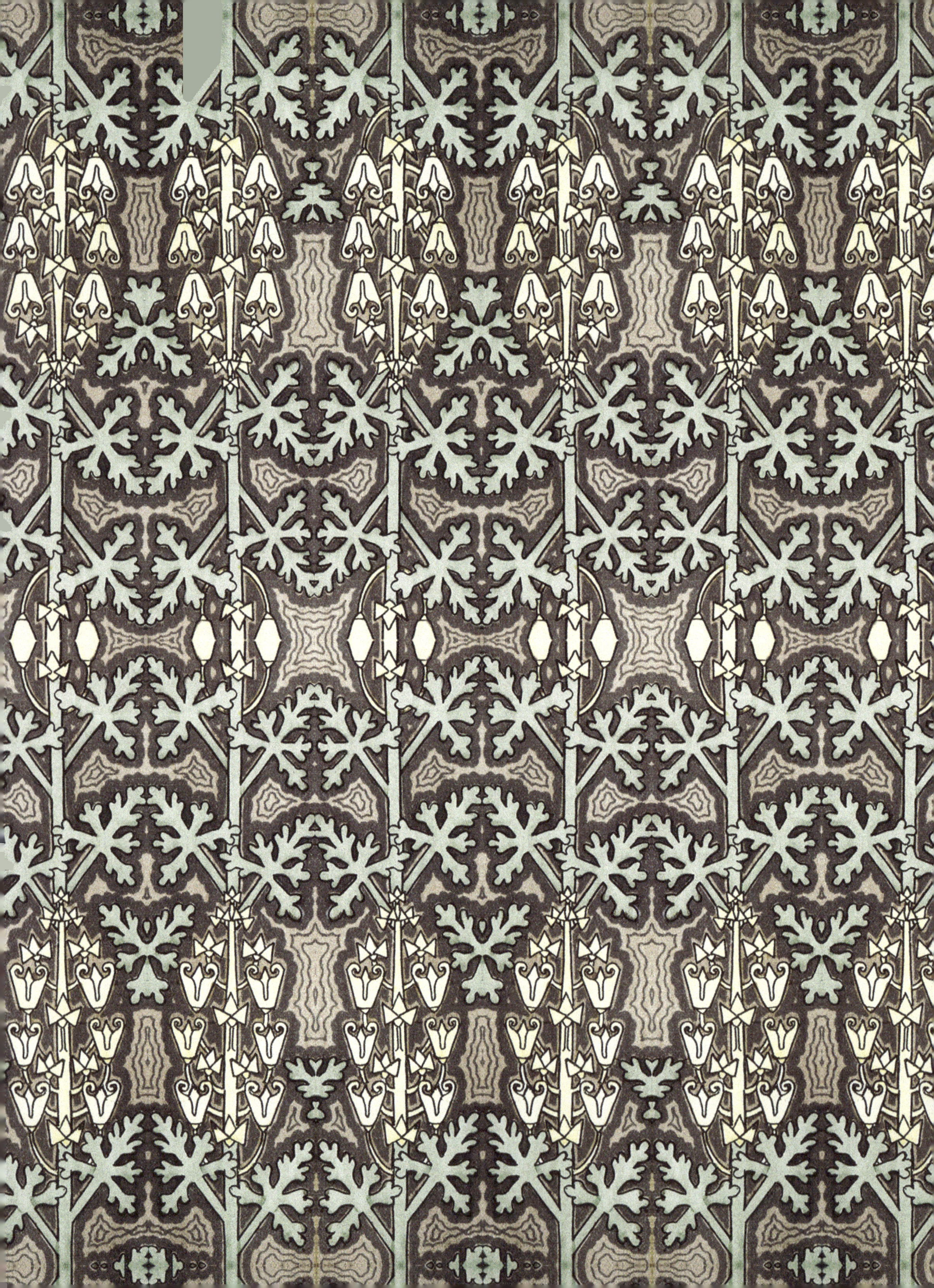

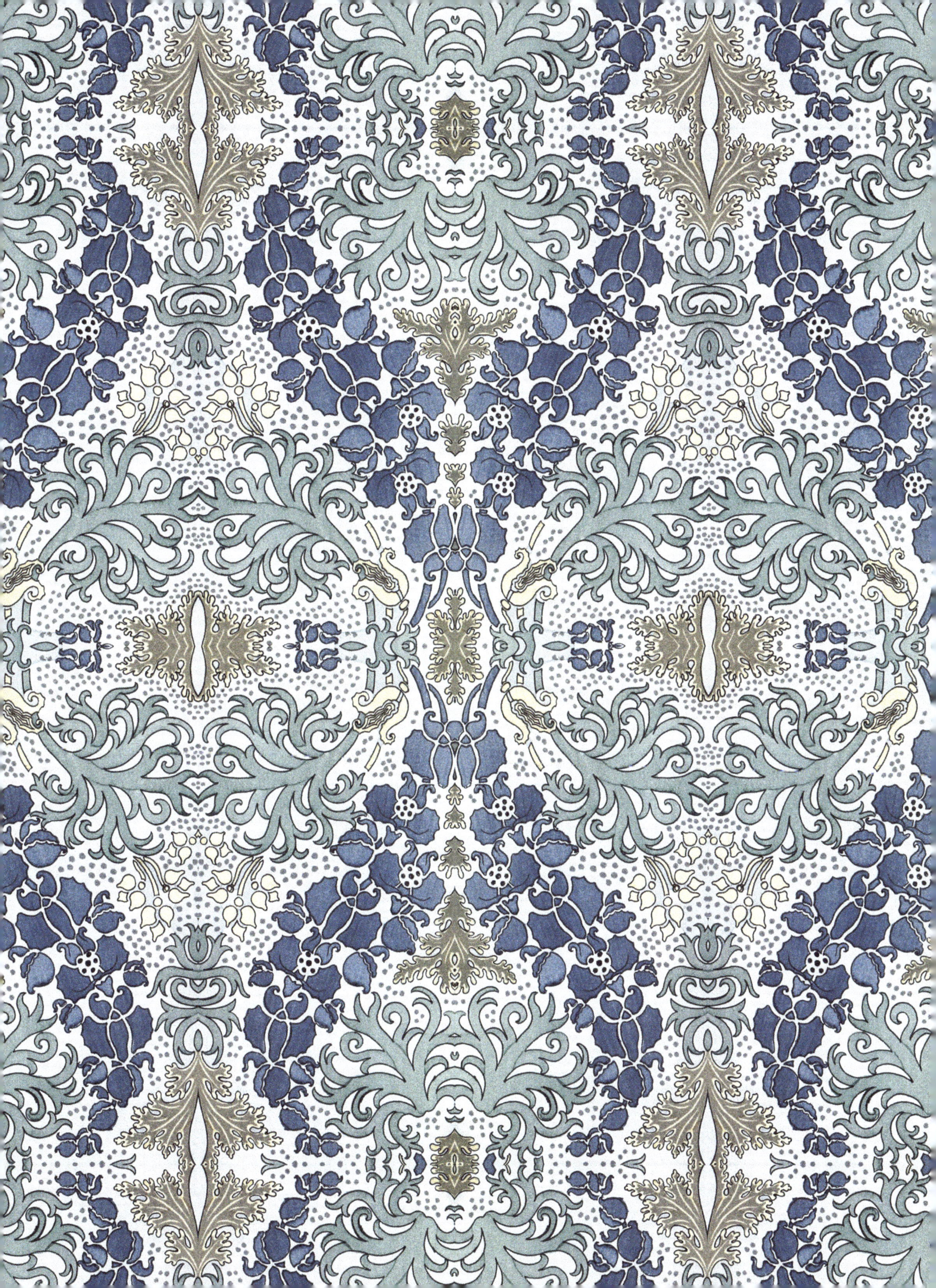

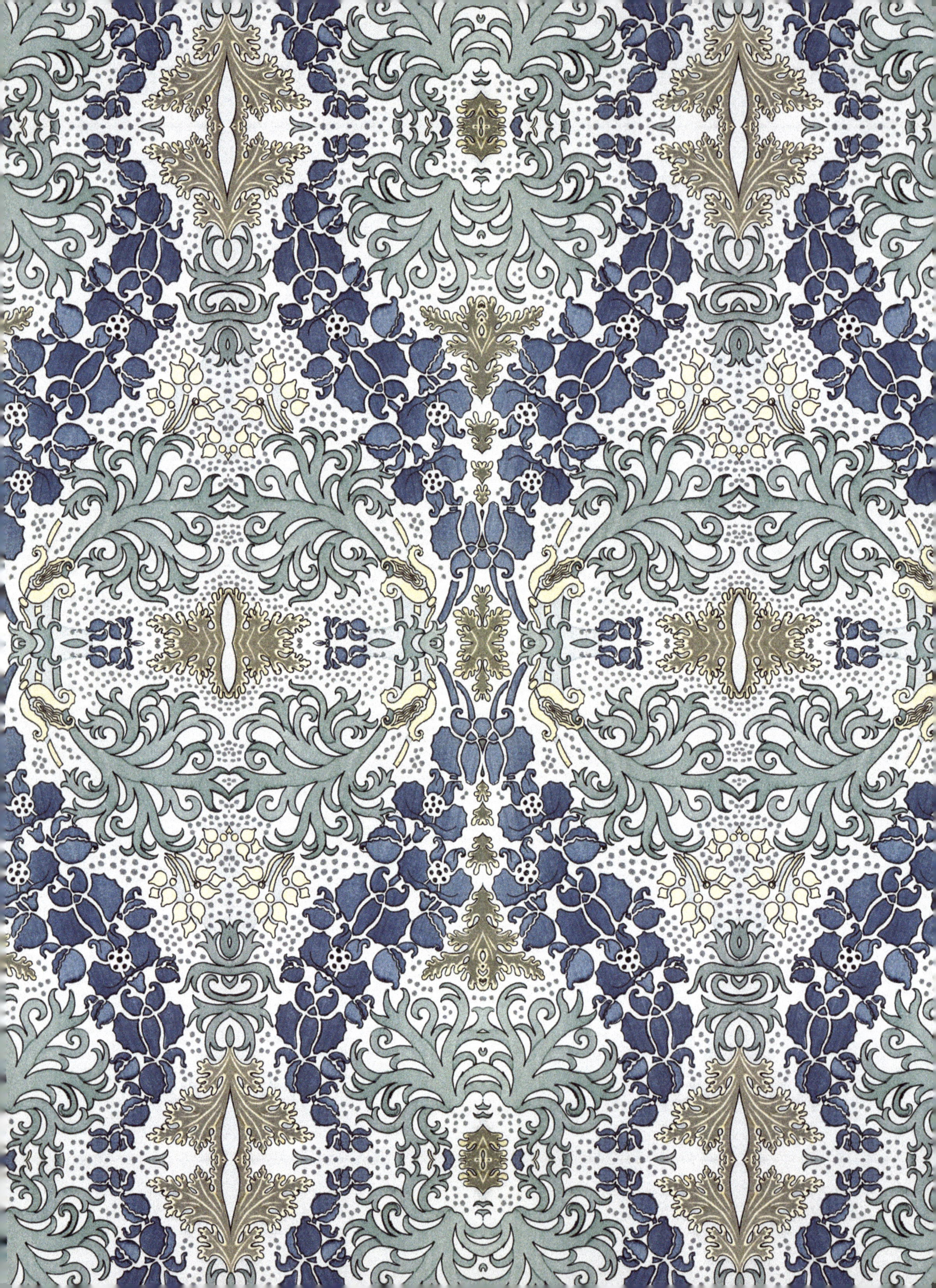

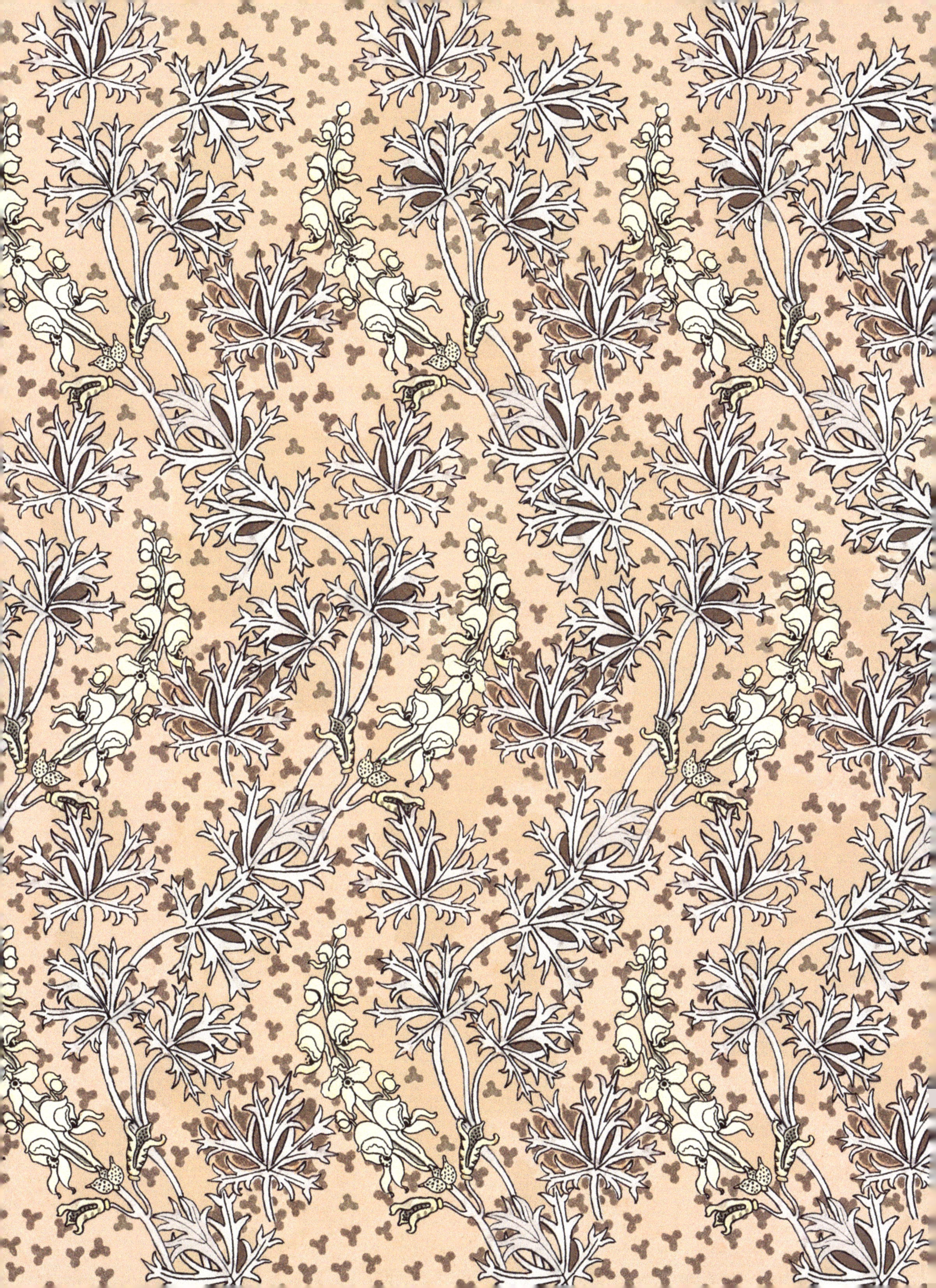

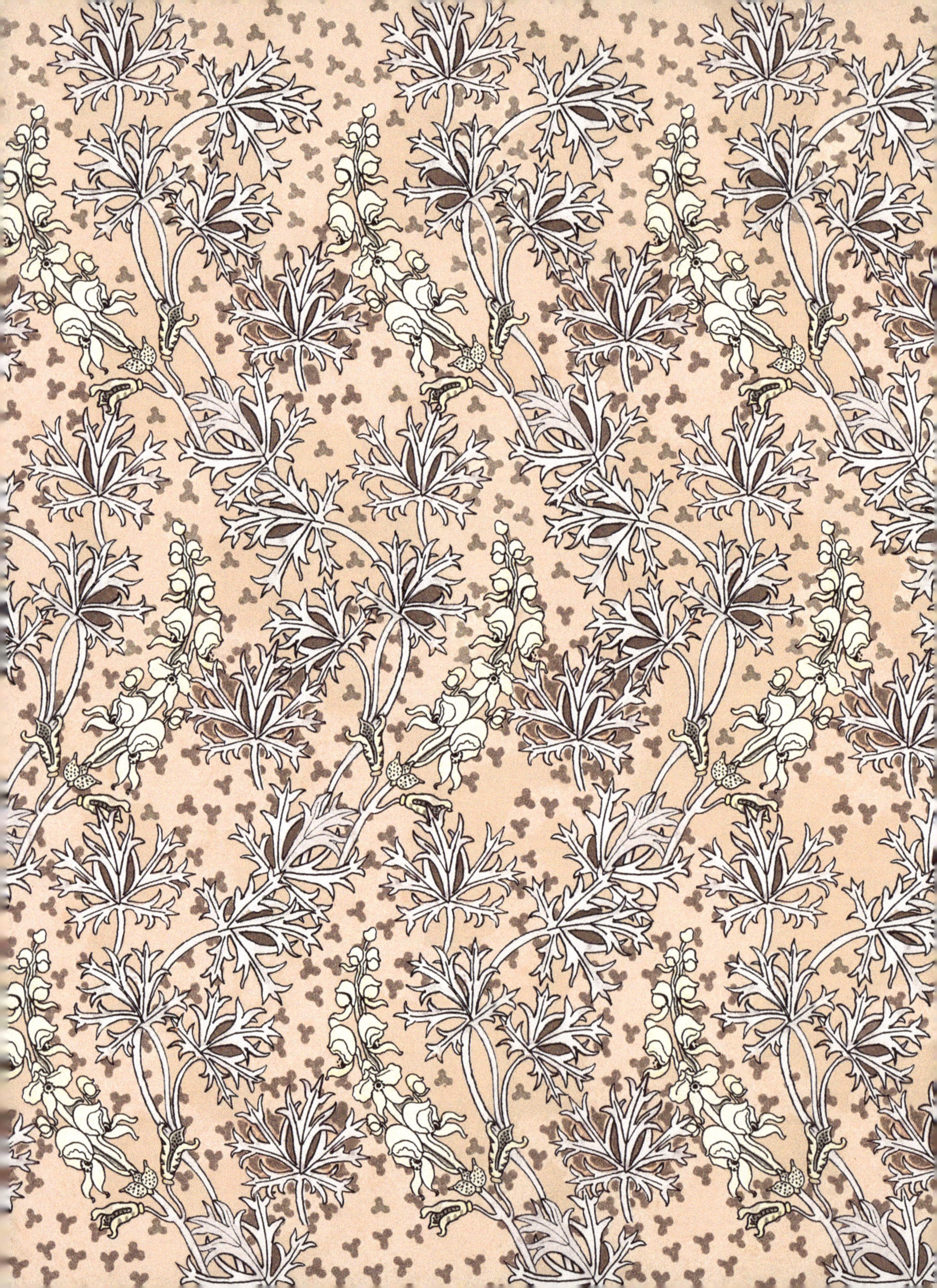

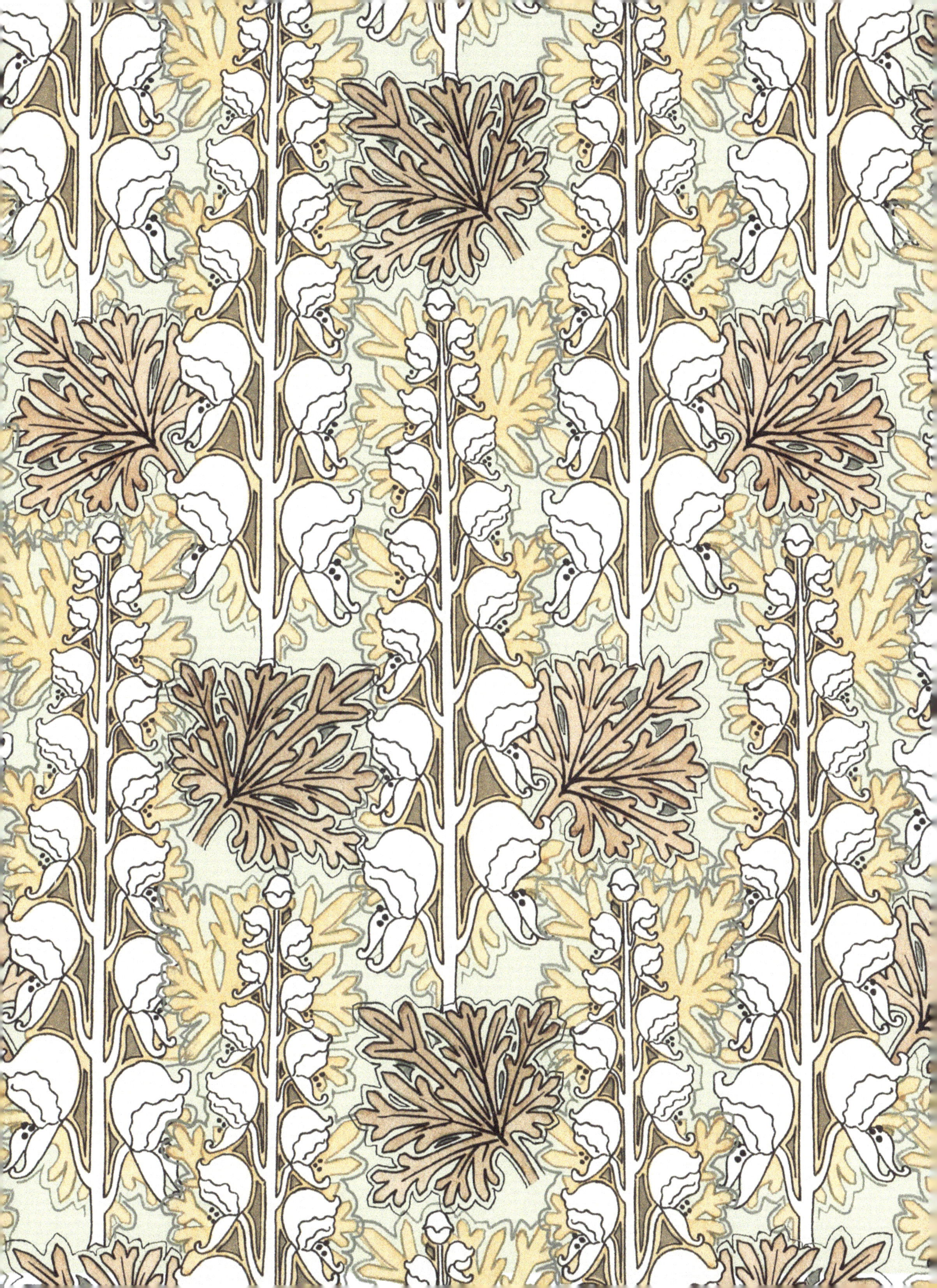

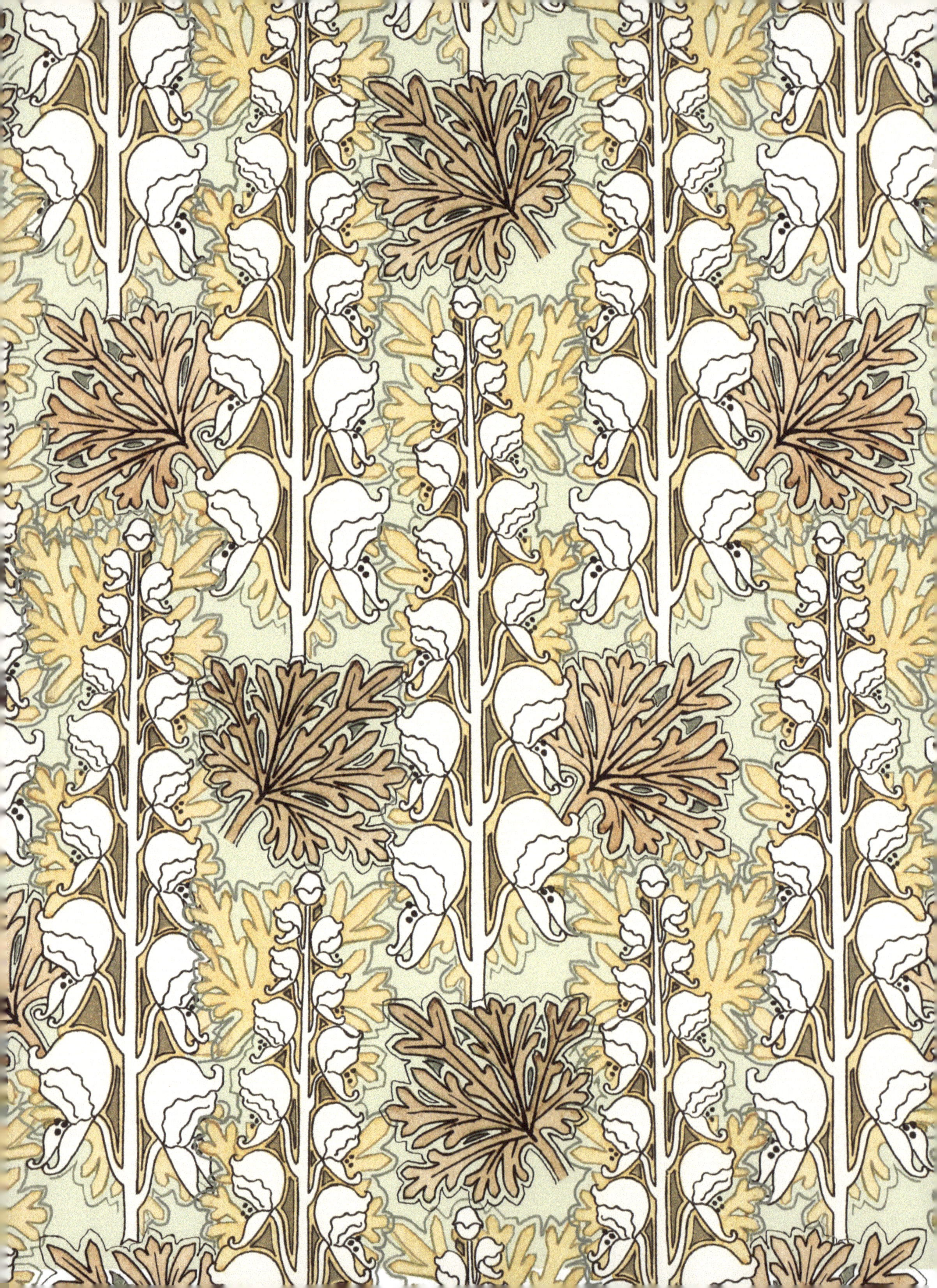

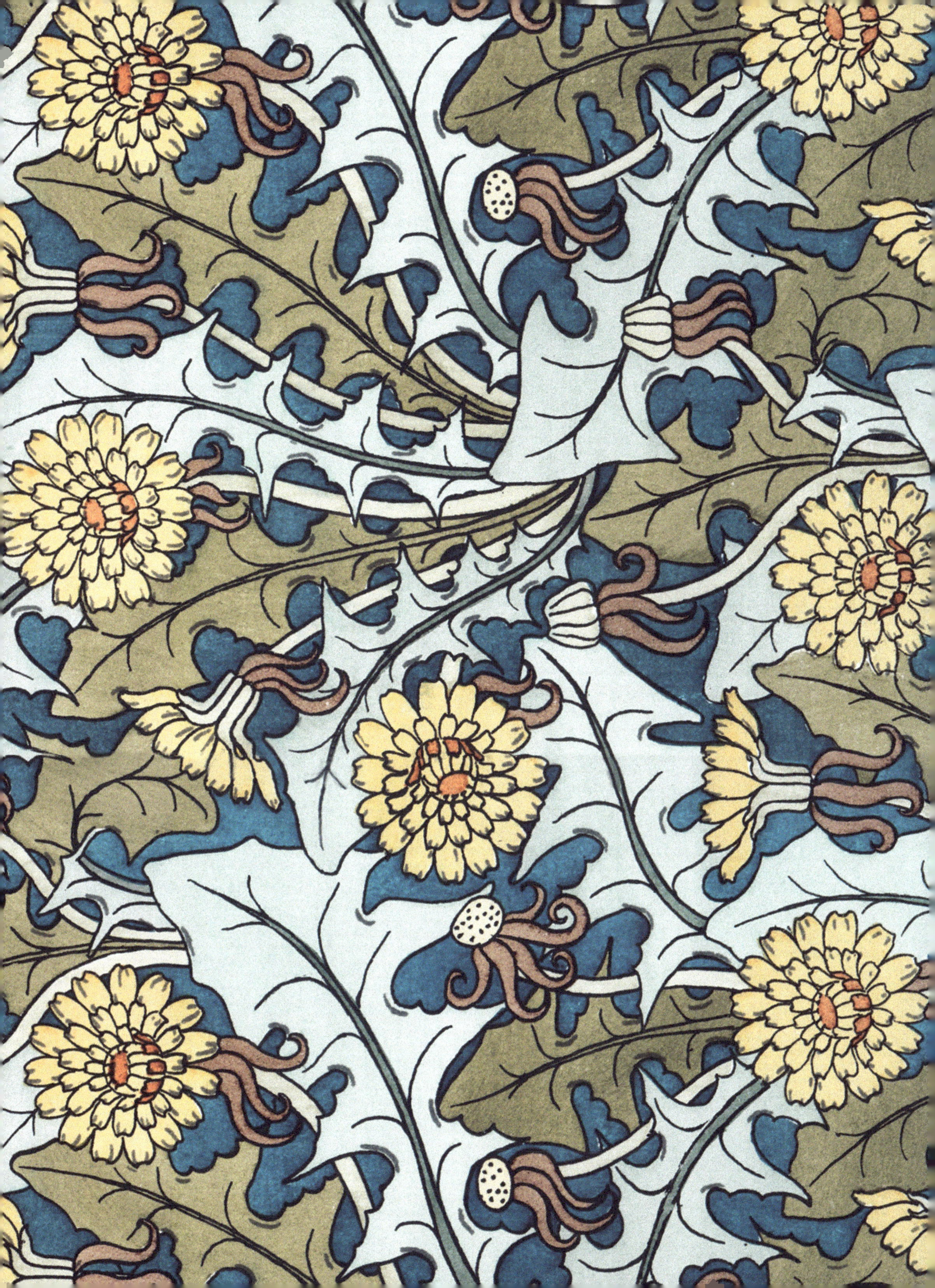

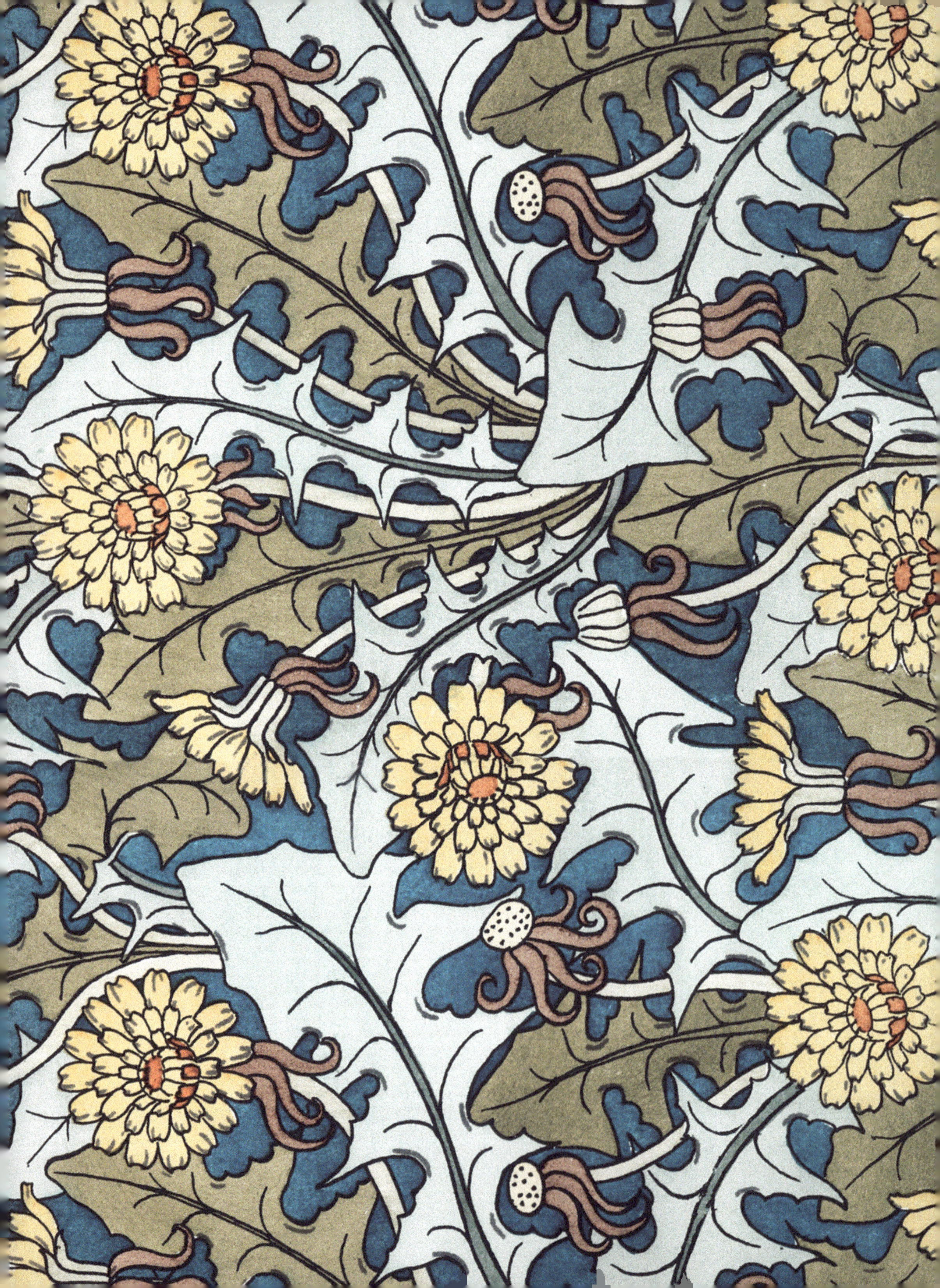

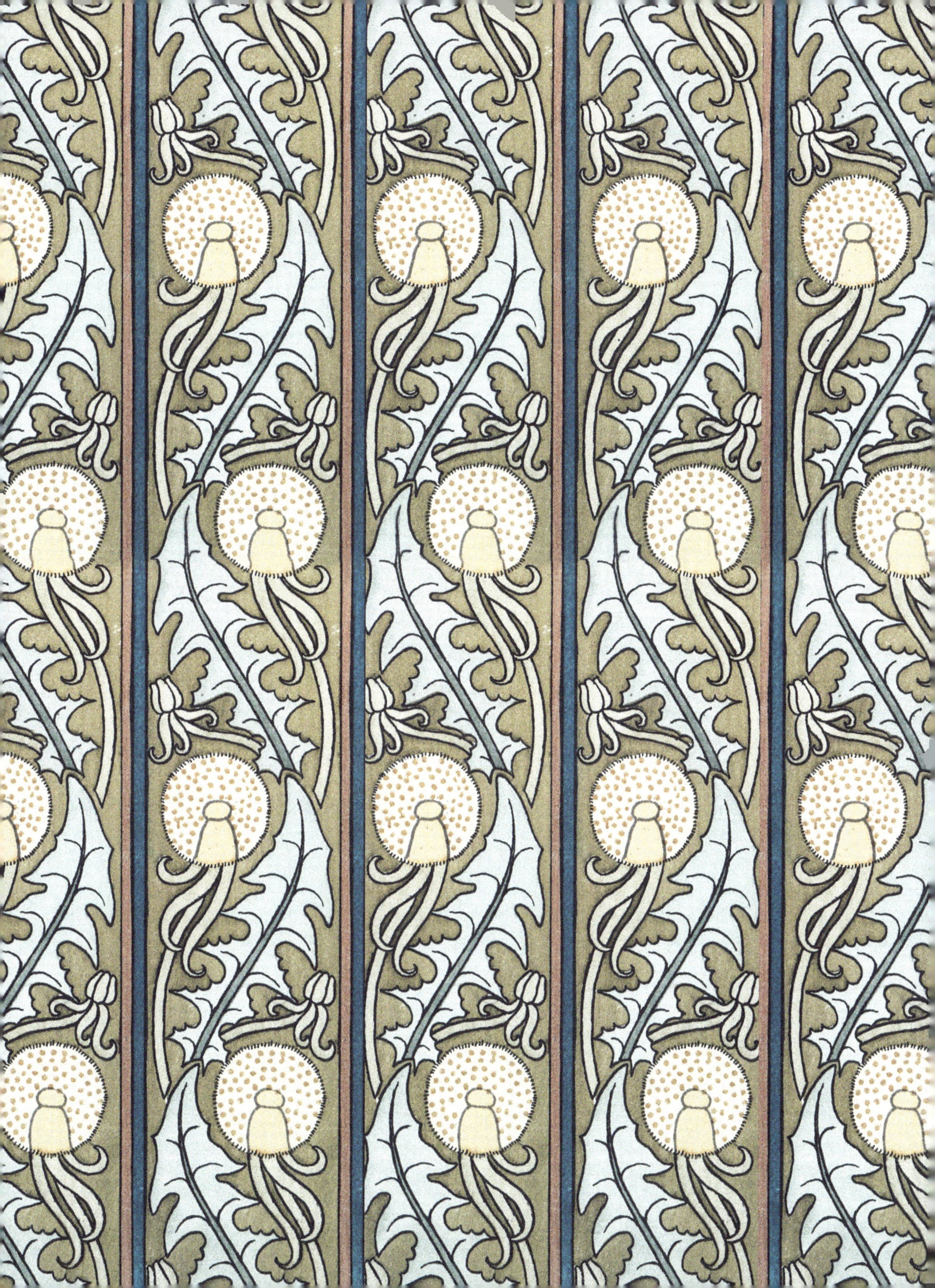

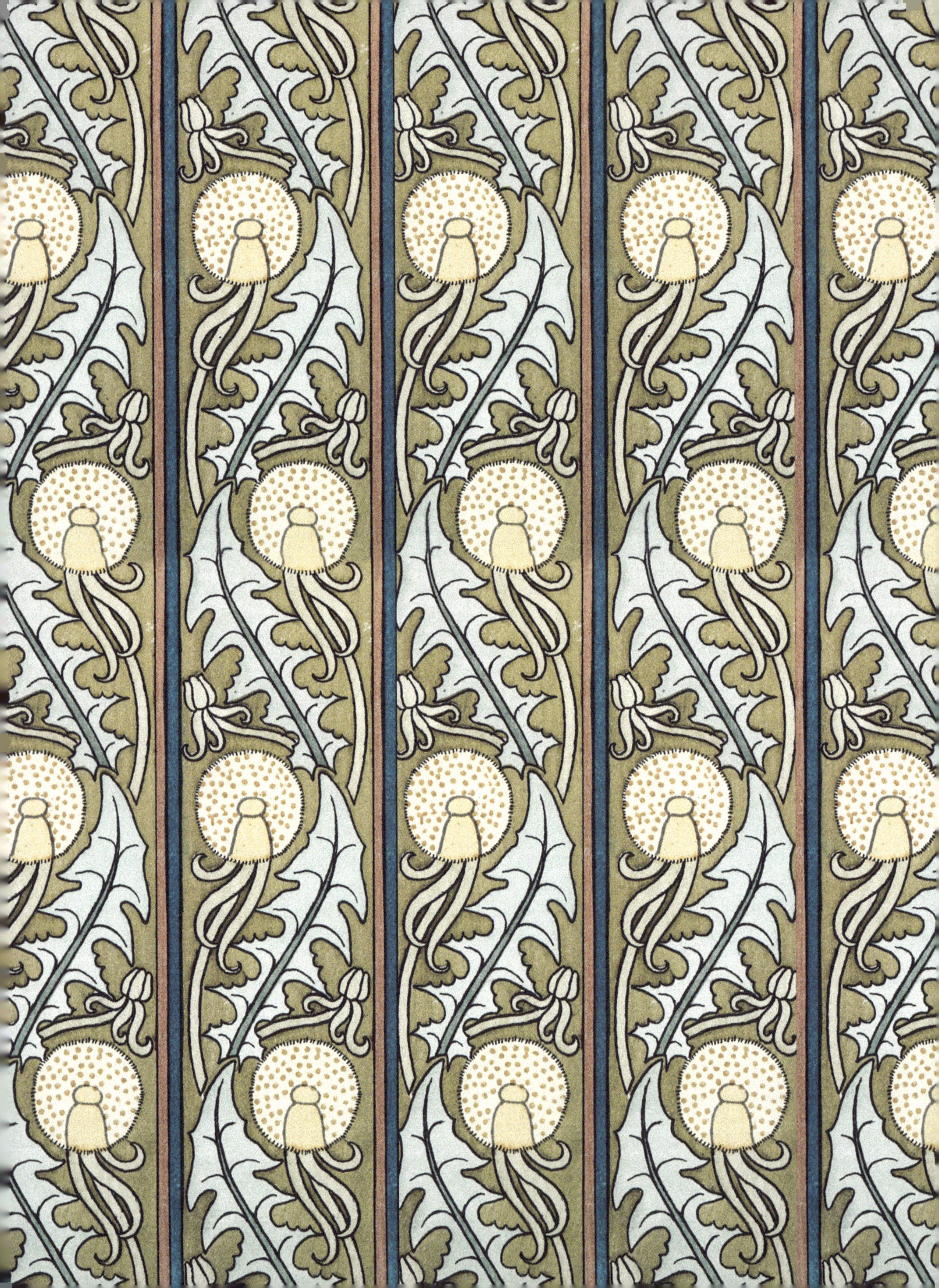

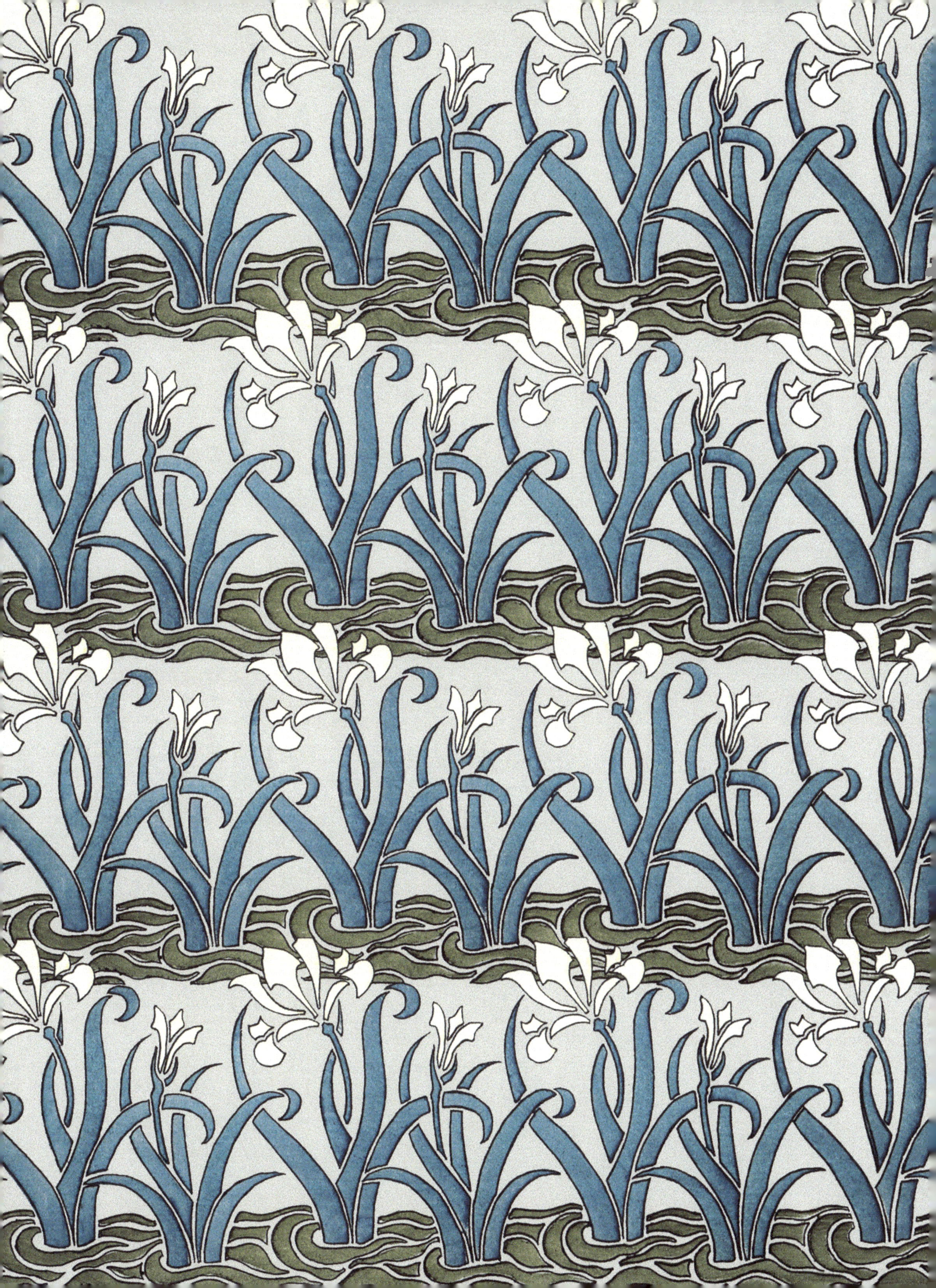

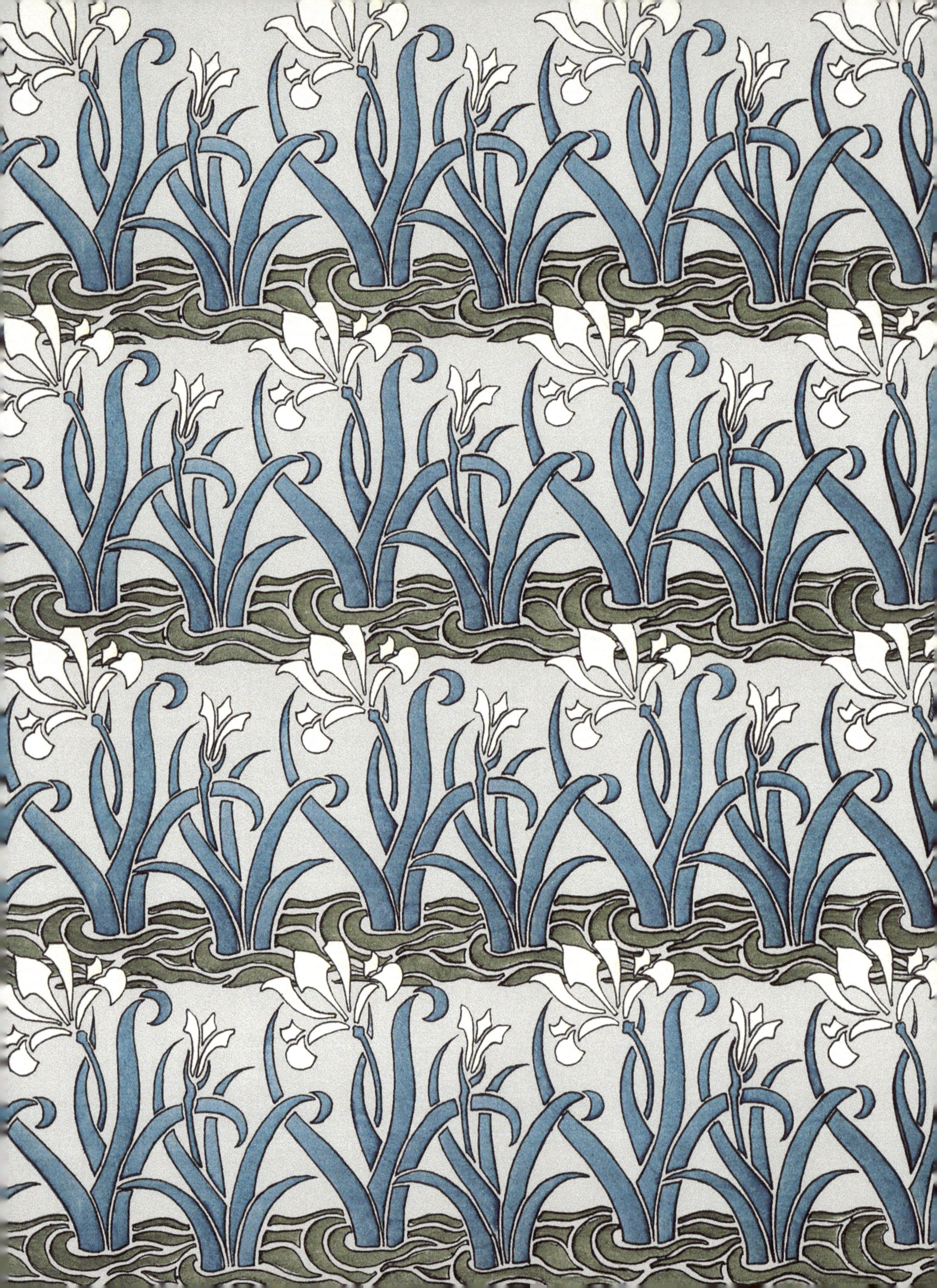

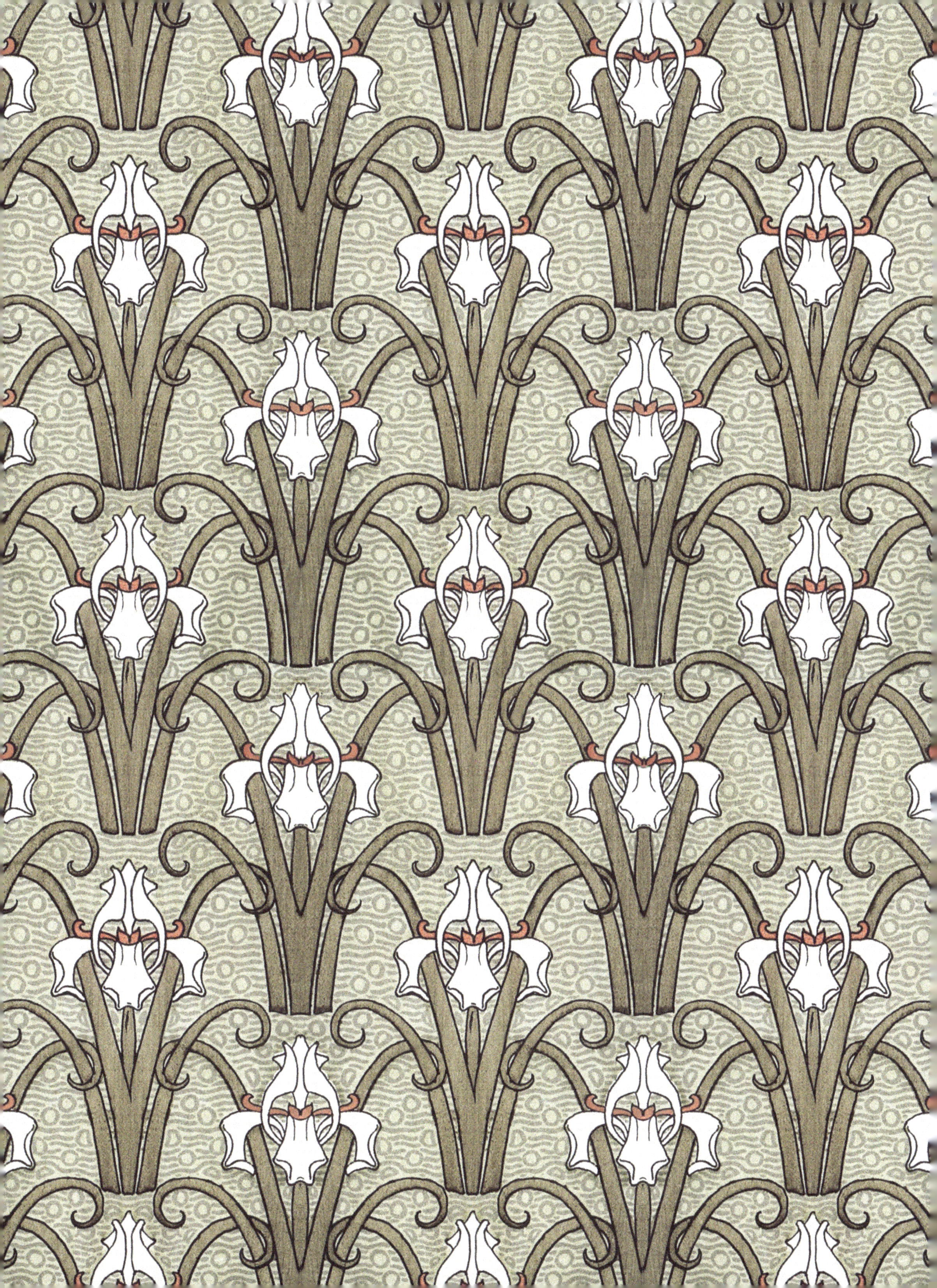

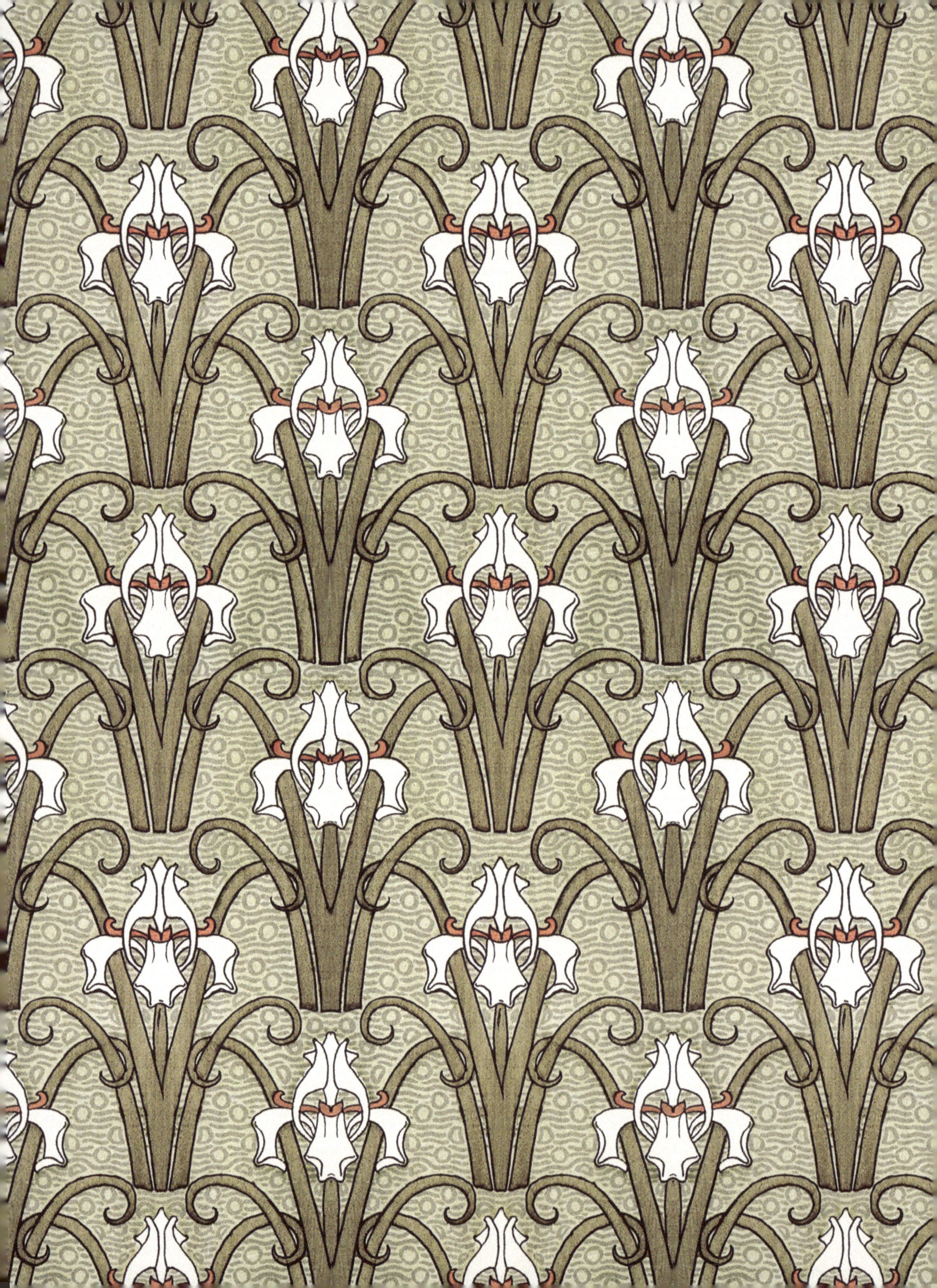

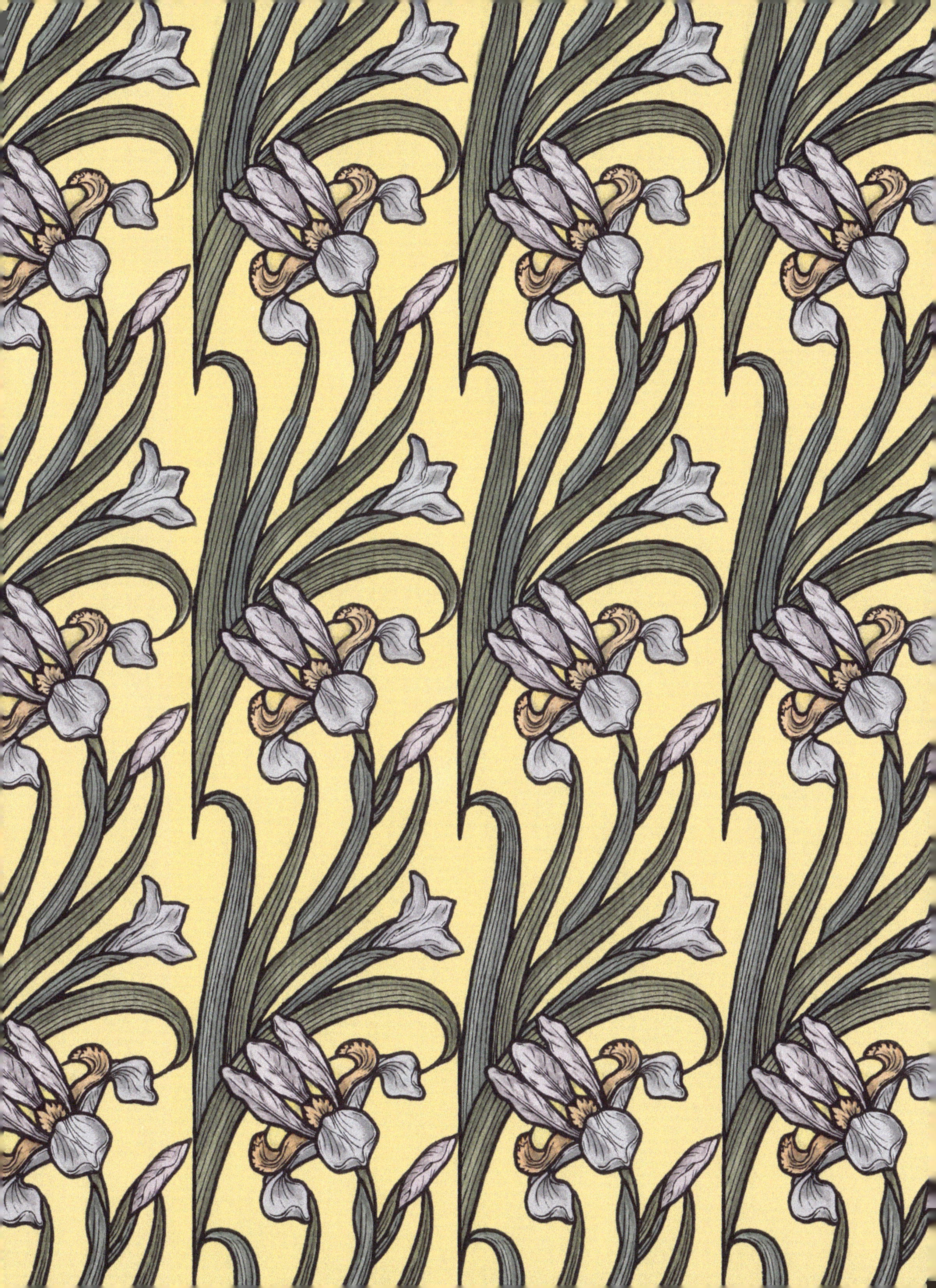

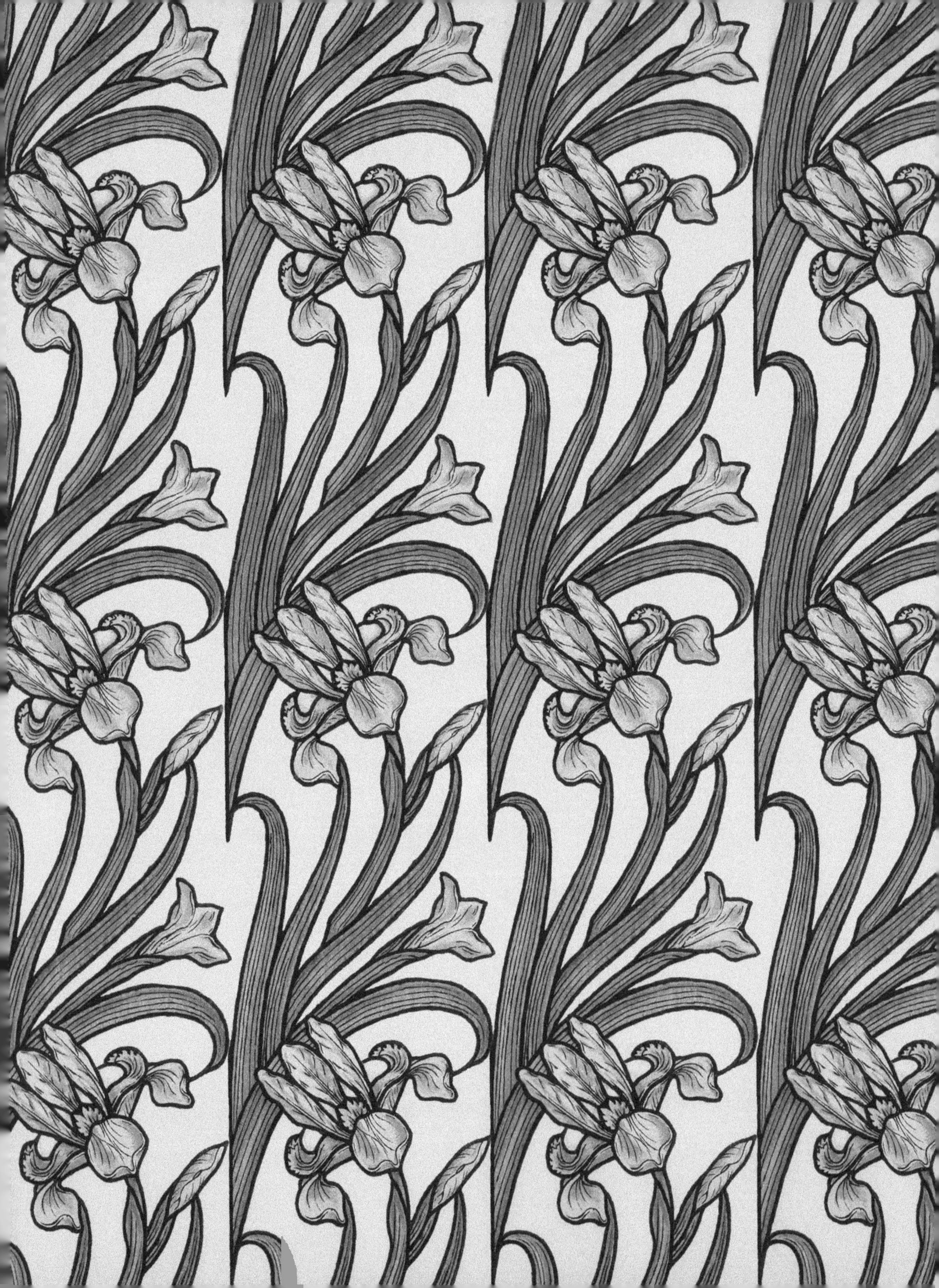

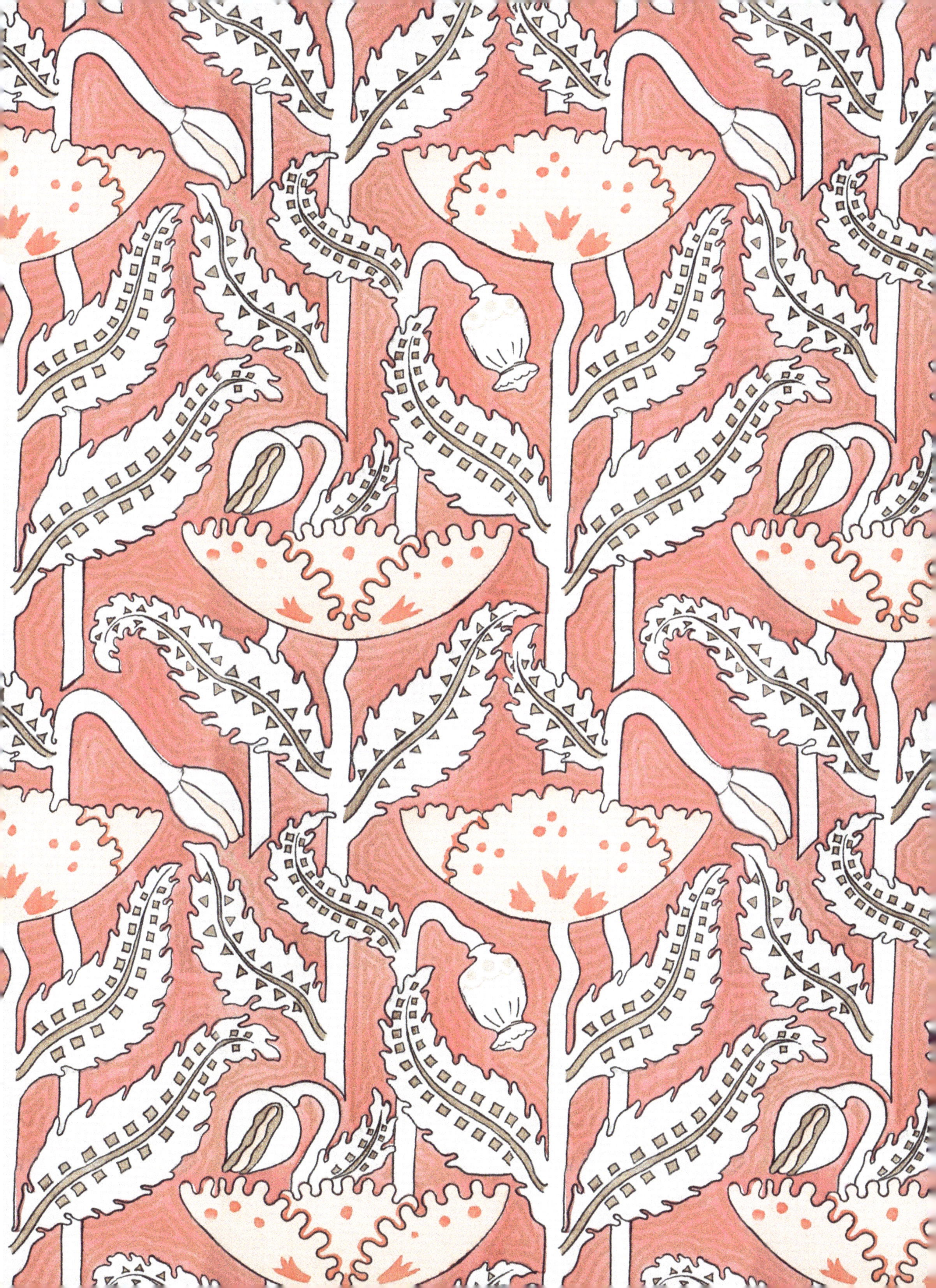

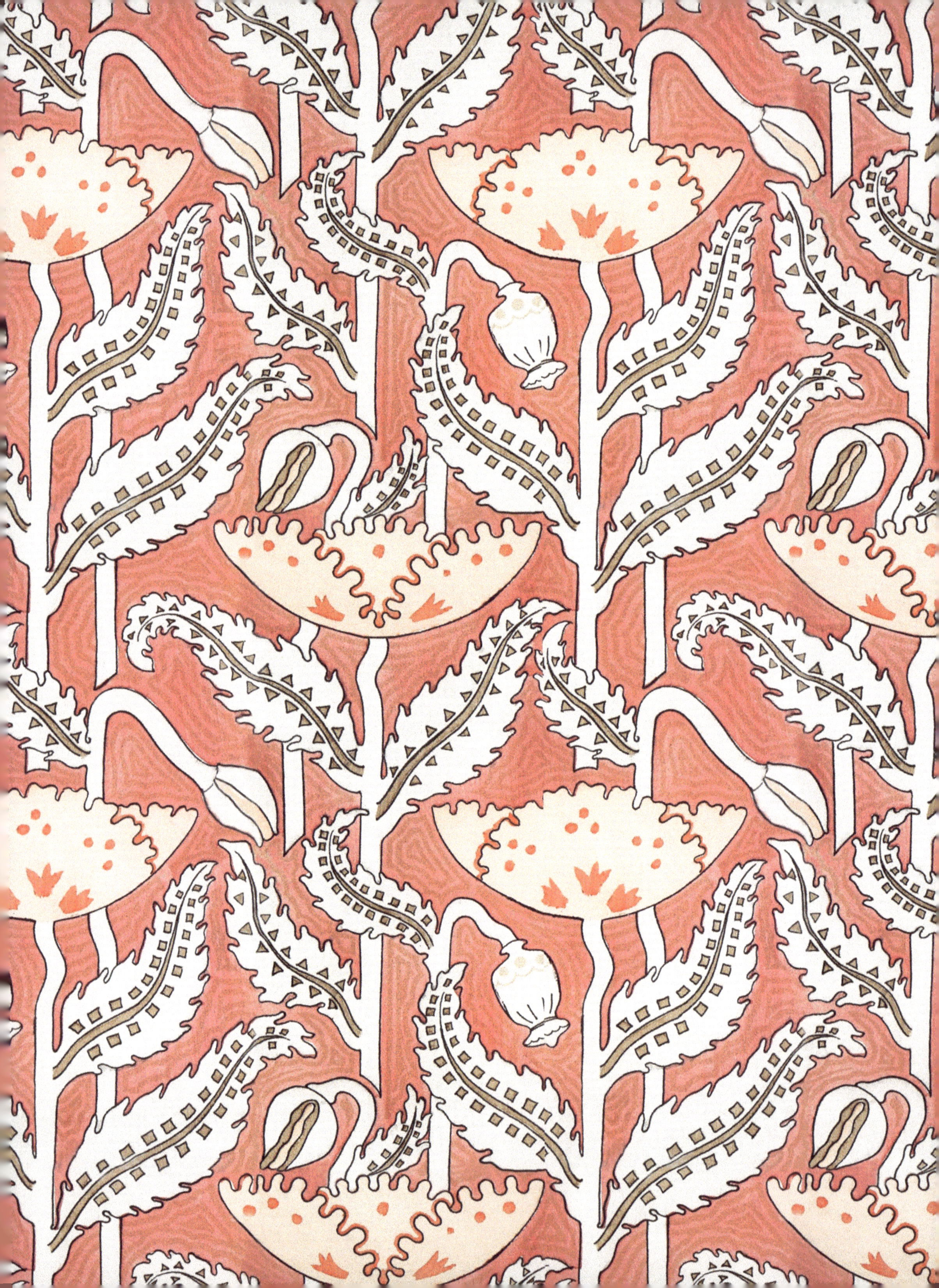

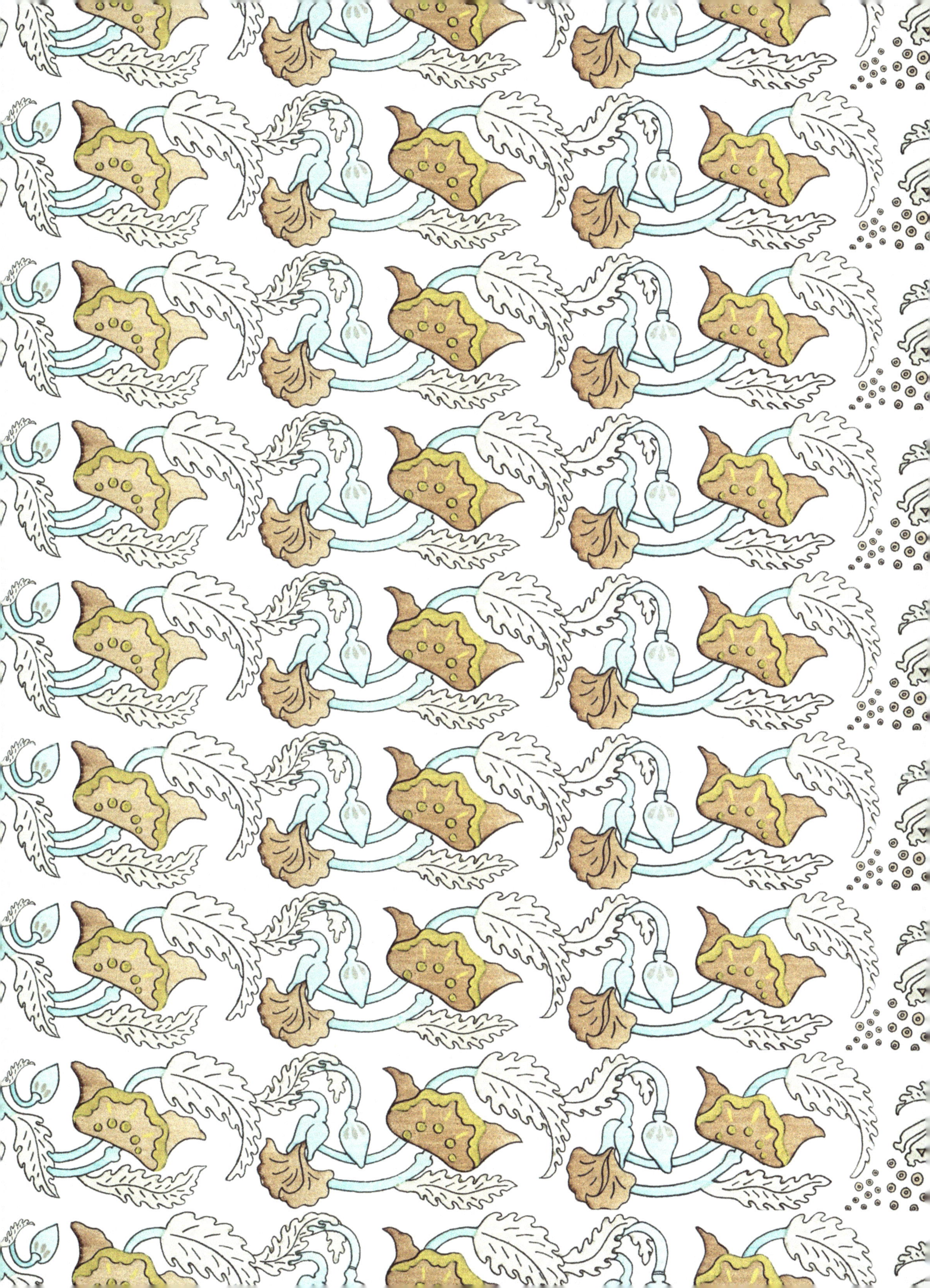

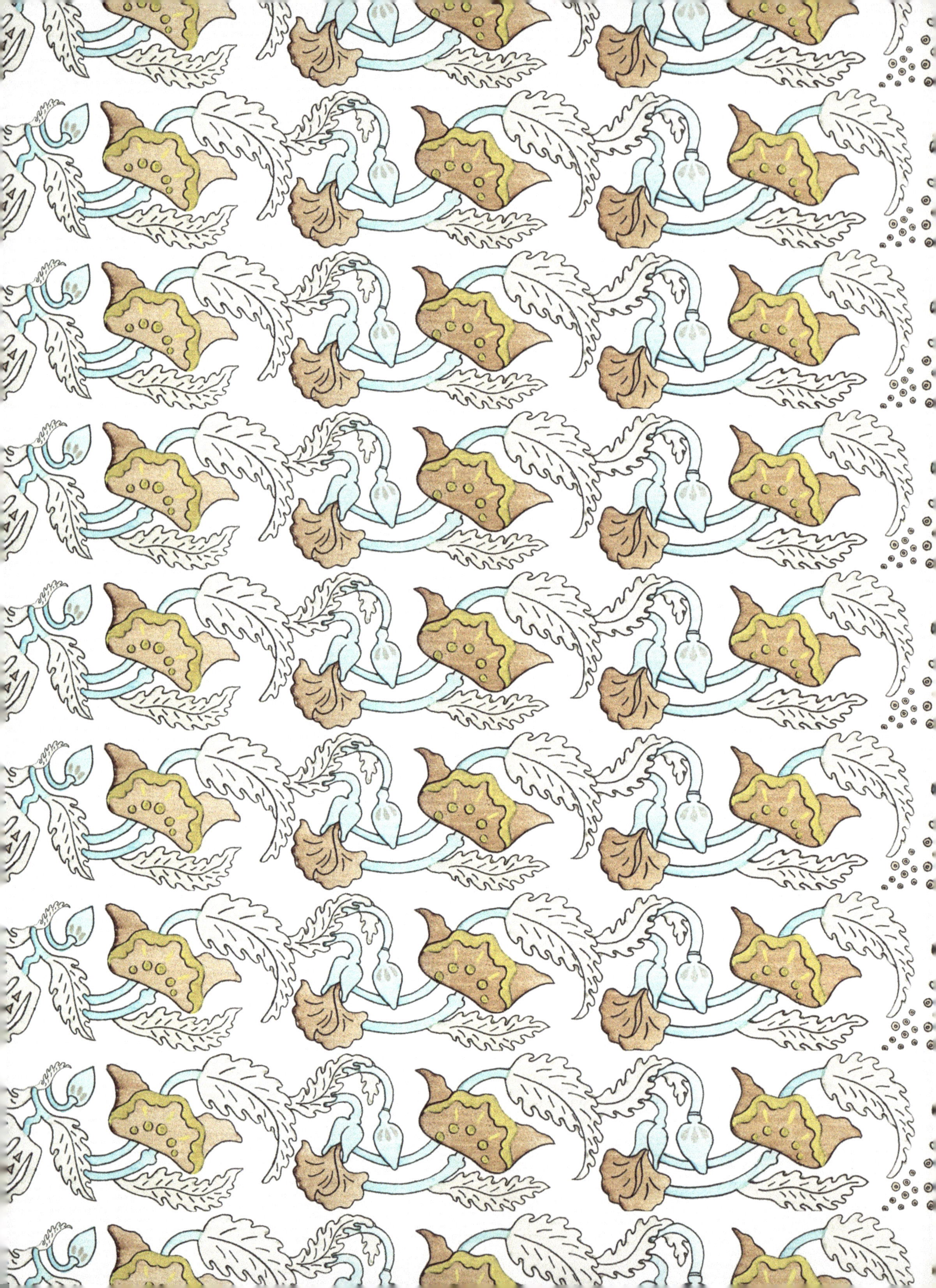

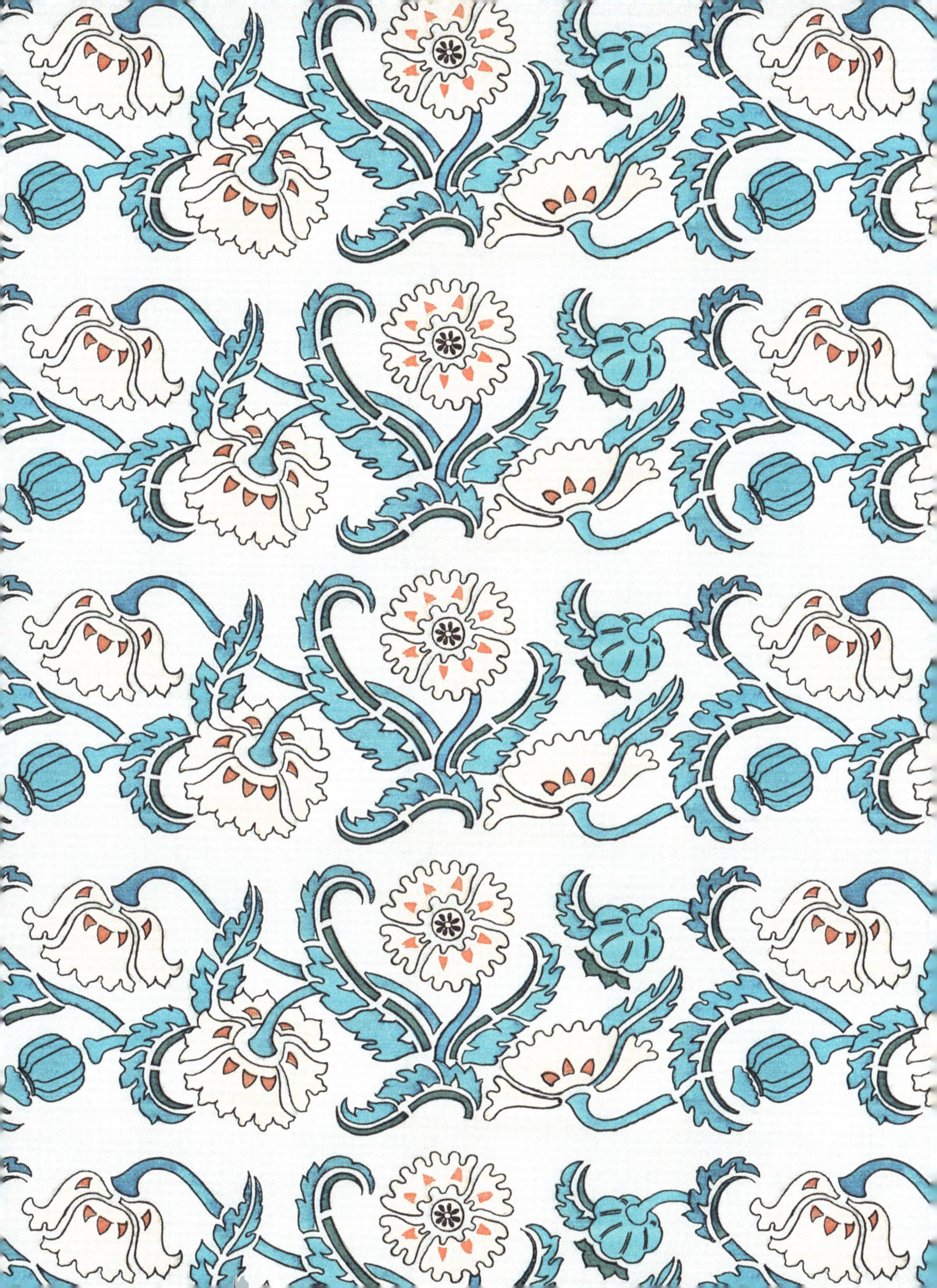

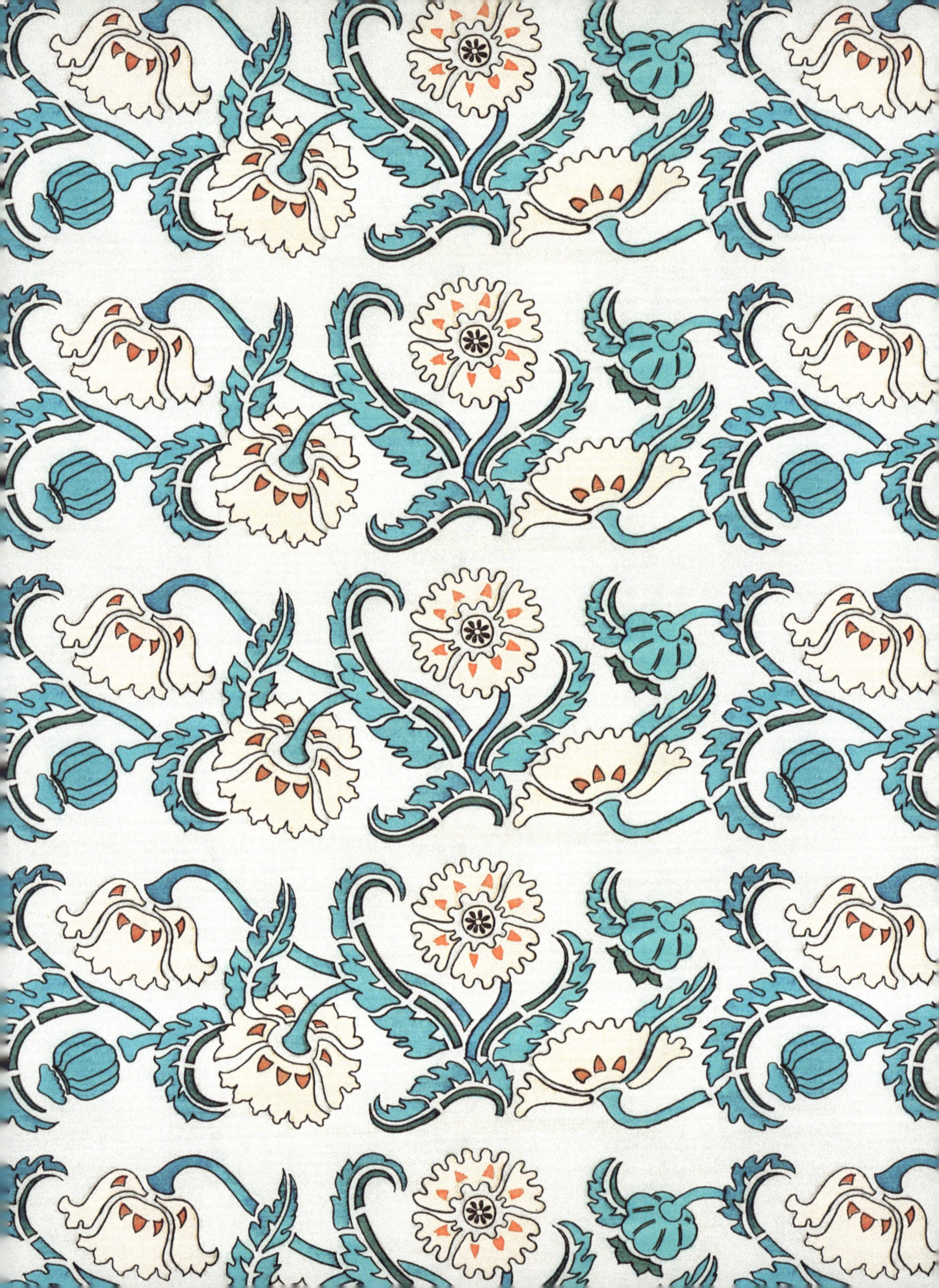

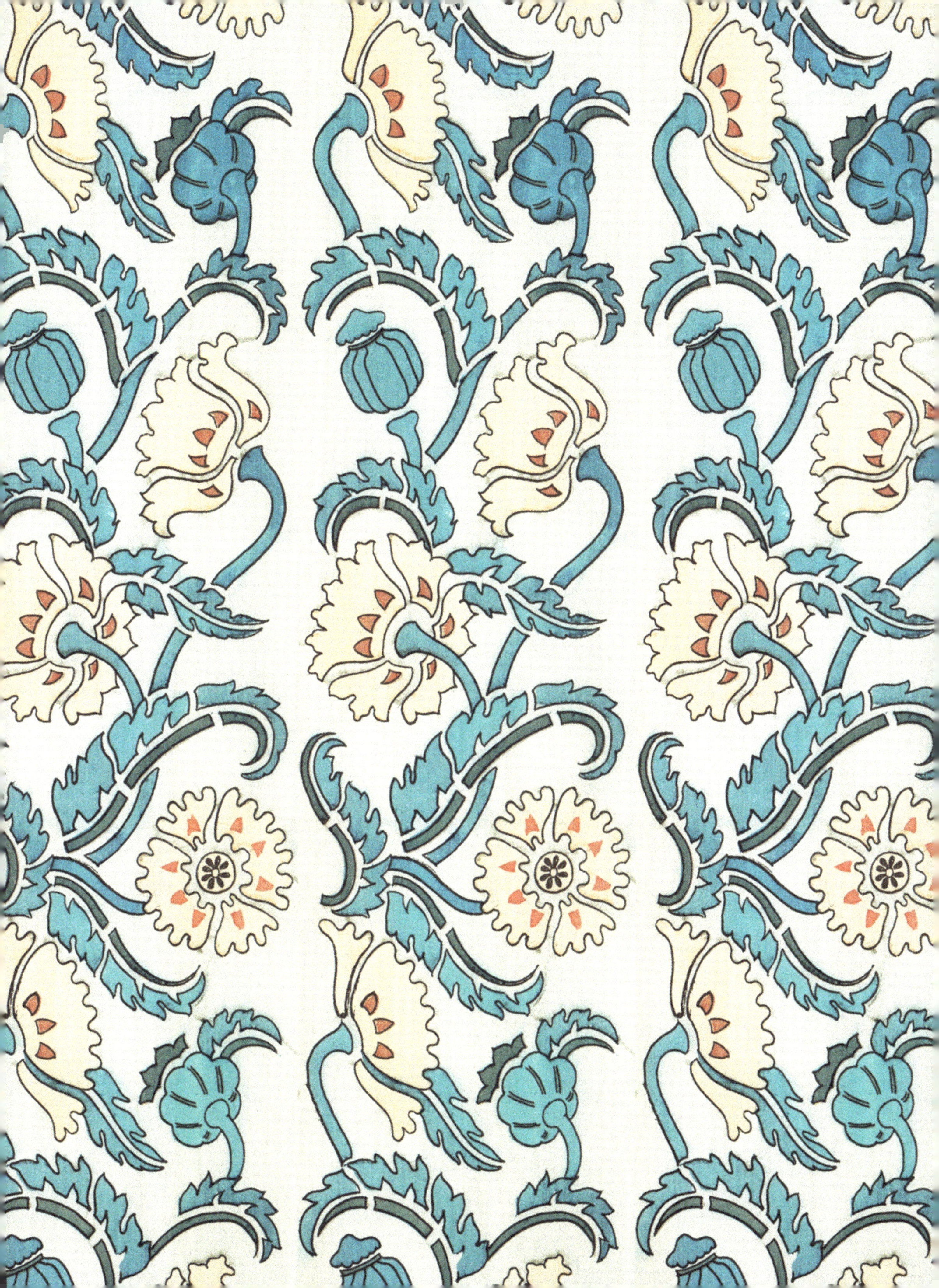

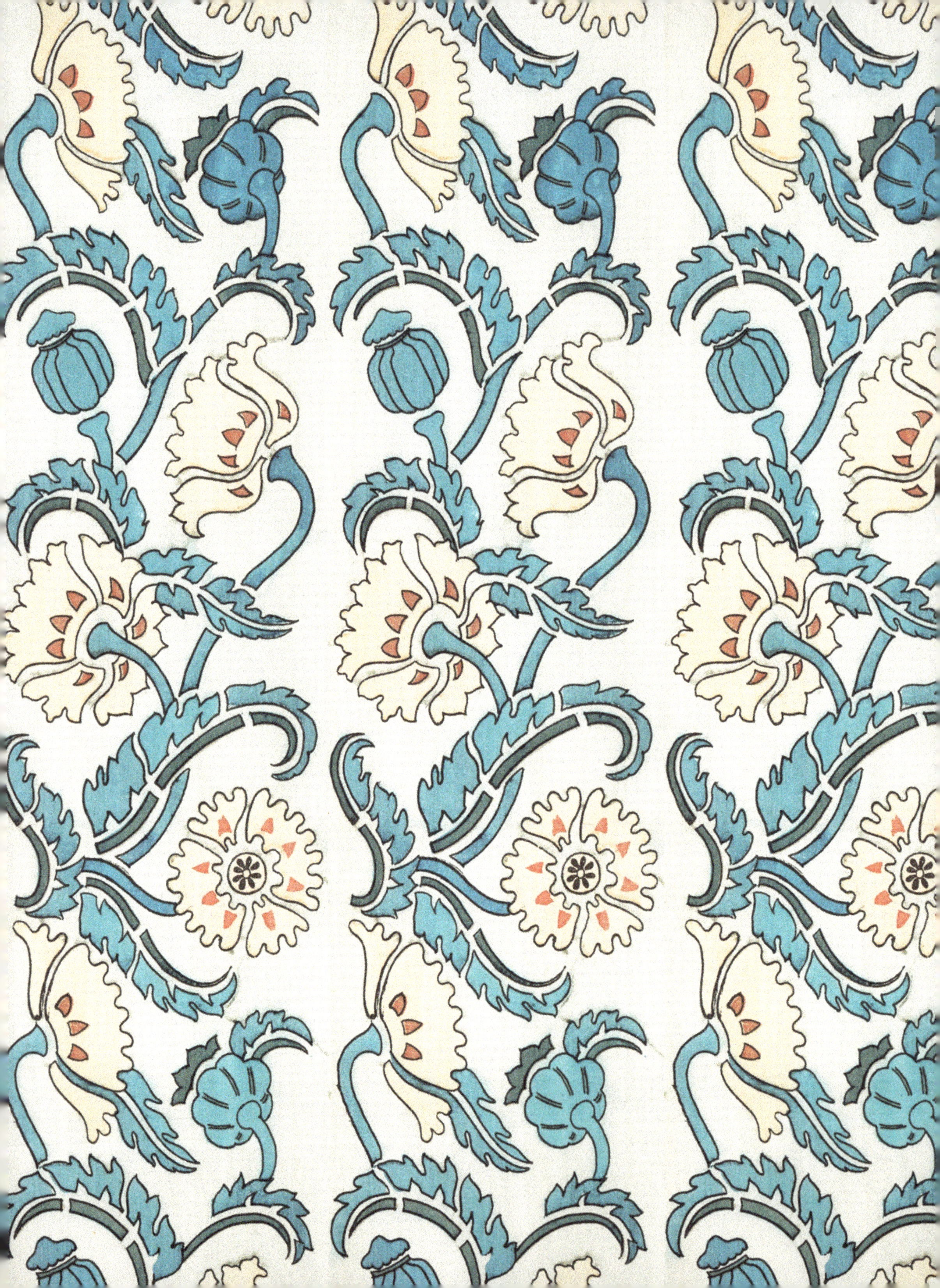